GUIDE
Menorca

A TOUR OF THE ISLAND

▼ TRIANGLE POSTALS

© 1997

TRIANGLE POSTALS S. L. Sant Lluís, Menorca

Photography

Jaume Serrat

Ricard Pla
Lluís Bertràn
Iñaki Relanzón
Melba Levick
Pere Sintes

Text

Joan Montserrat

Imma Planes *(Information and suggestions)*

Acknowledgements

Lluís Plantalamor (Museu de Menorca)
Fernando Contreras (Ecomuseu de Cap de Cavalleria)
Aeroclub Sant Lluís

Translation

Jina Monger

Grafic concept

Joan Barjau
Ricard Pla

Illustrations

Perico Pastor

Layout

Triangle Postals. S. L.

Cartograpy

Triangle Postals. S. L.

Colour separations

Tecnoart

Printed by

Industrias Gráficas Viking S.A.

Depósito legal

B.: 30.518 - 1997

ISBN

84-89815-18-6

Contents

MENORCA, AN ISLAND OF SURPRISES 5
  Geophysical features.......................... 6
  Water, light and wind 7
  Flora and fauna 8
  The sea and its riches 10

HISTORY AND SOCIOLOGY 14
  The Catalan conquest 15
  British and French domination 16
  Recent history 17
  Economy 19

PREHISTORIC MONUMENTS 20
  Burial caves 21
  Burial *navetes* 21
  Talaiots 22
  Taules 22

RURAL ARCHITECTURE 24

FÊTES AND FESTES 28

FROM EAST TO WEST 30
  Maó 30
  Es Castell 33
  Sant Lluís 33
  Alaior 34
  Es Mercadal and Fornells 35
  Ferreries 36
  Es Migjorn 36
  Ciutadella 37

THE WHOLE COASTLINE FROM THE AIR / EXCURSIONS
  I.   From Maó to Na Macaret 40
  II. From Arenal d'en Castell to Cala Pregonda 54
  III. From Cala Pilar to Macarella 68
  IV. From Cala Galdana to Cala en Porter 84
  V.   From Cales Coves to Cala Sant Esteve 96

GENERAL MAP 110

CAR TOURS 112
  1. From Maó to Son Parc 112
  2. From Alaior to Cap de Cavalleria 113
  3. Around Ciutadella 114
  4. From Es Mercadal to Cala Galdana 115
  5. South-eastern area 116

INFORMATION AND SUGGESTIONS 118
  Art and culture 118
  Handicrafts 121
  Antiques 121
  Festivities 122
  Sport 123
  Accommodation 125
  Gastronomy 126
  Transport 126
  Medical attention 127
  Useful telephones 127

Cala Macarelleta

An island of surprises

Even the briefest visit to Menorca tends to provide the curious traveller with an insight into the unique and surprising nature of the island's character.

This element of surprise has become a rare commodity in this day and age and is, therefore, for the visitor, one of the most rewarding first impressions.

The second largest and most northeastern of the Balearics, Menorca differs from the other islands in both climate and morphology. Throughout the course of history, successive changes of fortune have left their mark here, as have the diverse cultural influences of the many races who have occupied the island over the centuries. This turbulent past history has endowed Menorca with an original, distinctive character about which much has been written. The island not only offers a wealth of things to see, but also much food for thought and discussion.

Here, in the past, a high degree of independence existed between one township and another and, on occasions, this even degenerated into conflictive rivalry. Each centre of population sought to protect itself against loss of identity and living space by keeping its distance from its neighbours. In modern times, both the need for a more global territorial policy and improvements in transport and communications contributed to a rapprochement between them which put an end to the exaggerated insularity of these "islands" within an island.

In total contrast to this attitude, and perhaps as a result of the cultural and ethnic melting pot from which they descend, Menorcans have always been open and generous in their dealings with outsiders. Suffice it to say that, until quite recent

Grazing land

Cala Galdana

times, it was customary for front doors to be left unlocked at all times and this is, indeed, significant of the tranquil way of life, the *calma*, that has always been one of Menorca's main attractions.

It is not easy to maintain such a life-style when faced with the massive influx of tourists during the summer months, although the people of Menorca do strive to share it with their visitors and bear with good grace the difficulties that inevitably arise when the seventy thousand inhabitants of the island find their numbers more than doubled. If the service industries sometimes appear inadequate, it can only be attributed to the disproportionate demands made upon them. The island's resources must be administered with care in order to ensure the continued survival of these privileged surroundings.

In recent years, the inhabitants of the islands have become increasingly preoccupied with the protection of their environment. Until a few years ago, opposition to development projects in Menorca had been almost exclusively limited to minority groups who foresaw the irremediable damage that could result from indiscrimate urbanization. (The *Grup Ornitològic Balear*, a local group dedicated to the conservation of nature and the environment, is one of the oldest and most active organizations of its kind in the country). Now, however, there is a unanimous desire to reconcile the interests of the conservationists with those of the tourist industry. Some sectors remained unconvinced of the importance of a protected environment until the recent concession by the United Nations of the **Reserve of the Biosphere** denomination.

Another decisive step, along the same lines, has been the *Llei d' Espais Naturals* legislation which guarantees different levels of protection for almost the entire island. Between those classified as *Àrees Naturals d' Especial Interès* or *Àrees Rurals d' Interès Paisatgístic*, (local equivalent of Sites of Special Scientific Interest), altogether nineteen zones have been included which gives a clear indication of the extent of the natural wealth of the island.

Geophysical features

In the south of the Gulf of Lyon, Menorca is situated practically in the centre of the western Mediterranean, at a point almost equidistant

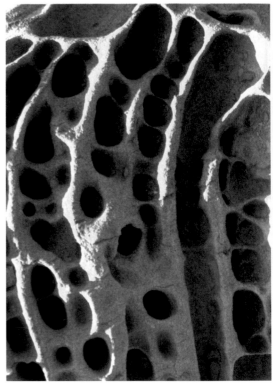

Erosion by wind

between Marseille and Algiers in a north-south direction, and Castelló de la Plana on the Spanish mainland and Oristano on the isle of Sardinia in an east-west direction. The area of the island measures 701 km^2., the perimeter 290 km., and 48 km. is the longest distance between one end of the island and the other. The four most extreme points are, to the north Cap de Cavalleria; to the south Illa de l'Aire; to the east Cap de Sa Mola; and to the west, Cap de Bajolí. The distance between Ciutadella and Alcúdia, the closest point on the island of Mallorca, is 50 km.

An imaginary line drawn from Maó harbour, across the island, to Algaiarens would coincide with a natural division of the land which varies greatly between the north and the south. Above this line we find the island's oldest terrain which, in part, pertains to the Paleozoic insular shelf and partly to the Triassic, Jurassic and Cretaceous eras. This combination results in an interesting contrast of colours and textures. It is an area of gently rolling hills, including Monte Toro (358 m.), S'Enclusa (274 m.), and Santa Àgueda (264 m.), the three highest points on the island.

Rural scene

A wide strip of Miocenic terrain overlapped the southernmost extreme of this area, forming a flat limestone surface. Later, torrents from the north eroded the soil and formed channels that remain today as the small, but deep, ravines or gorges that are characteristic of this part of the island. Here in the *migjorn*, the south of Menorca, the rock is calcareous and the sand white, whereas, in the *tramuntana*, or north, the rock is siliceous with traces of sandstone, slate and shale.

Water, light and wind

The animal and vegetable life of the island has adapted to the conditions of the subsoil and to the availability of water. The supply of drinking water has preoccupied Menorcans since the beginning of time, as is demonstrated by the prehistoric *cocons*, shallow niches excavated in the rock, and the cisterns and tanks of more recent times. The collection of rain water has always been imperative as there are few natural sources. Principally, they are found in the south of the island, where the more permeable subsoil permits the formation of underground reserves.

Fortunately, the climate is very humid as compared to the rest of the archipelago. The visitor who has only seen Menorca during the dry summer months can hardly imagine the intense verdancy of the rest of the year. Except for years of generalized drought, the regularity of the rainfall and the abundant winter dews compensate for the summer dryness. Autumn, unknown here as a season, is replaced by the *primavera d'hivern*, or winter's spring. The mildness of the temperatures and the virtual absence of the deciduous trees that, in other latitudes, are the first indicators of the proximity of winter, add to the spring-like atmosphere that can be enjoyed here in October and November.

Another decisive characteristic of Menorca's climate is the constant presence of the wind. As there are no natural obstacles to stop it, the island is at the mercy of gusts from all directions. Those from the north are the most dominant and, among them, the fierce *tramuntana*, the strongest and most insistent, reaches speeds of between 35 and 90 km. per hour. It has spectacular effects on the environment: bowing and reshaping trees and bushes in its path, hampering

Monte Toro

AT 358 METRES ABOVE SEA LEVEL, MONTE TORO IS THE GEOGRAPHIC CENTRE OF THE ISLAND AND A PLACE OF PILGRIMAGE. ITS LOCATION MAKES IT A PERFECT VANTAGE POINT FROM WHICH THE ENTIRE COASTLINE OF THE ISLAND CAN BE SEEN AND, ON CLEAR DAYS, MALLORCA IS VISIBLE ON THE HORIZON TO THE SOUTH-EAST. ONCE IT WAS FORTIFIED TO PROTECT THE ISLANDERS FROM THE INCURSIONS OF BERBER PIRATES AND TODAY IT IS A SPIRITUAL REFUGE DEDICATED TO OUR LADY DEL TORO, PATRON SAINT OF MENORCA WHOSE IMAGE, SO LEGEND HAS IT, WAS DISCOVERED HERE BY A FRIAR FOLLOWING THE SIGNS PASSED ONTO HIM BY A SILVER-HOOFED BULL. THE MONASTERY IS INHABITED TODAY BY FRANCISCAN NUNS. THE HILL-TOP IS SOMEWHAT CLUTTERED WITH A PROFUSION OF COMMUNICATION AERIALS AND ANTENNAS, AND A RATHER PERPLEXING MEMORIAL TO THE DEAD OF THE NORTH-AFRICAN WAR.

THE MOUNTAIN'S NAME IS DERIVED FROM THE PRE-ROMANESQUE NOUN *TOR*, ORIGIN OF THE CATALAN *TURÓ* OR HILL. THE ARABS CALLED IT *AL THOR* WHICH HAD THE SAME SIGNIFICANCE. IT IS POSSIBLE TO WALK TO THE TOP FOLLOWING A FOOTPATH ON THE NORTH SIDE AND, ON THIS SAME SLOPE, AT THE SITE OF THE ENZELL SPRING, MENORCA'S ONLY MINERAL-WATER BOTTLING PLANT HAS RECENTLY BEEN INSTALLED.

work on the land and at sea, and depositing harmful salt on crops and orchards. In compensation, the *tramuntana* brings with it an abundance of blue skies, clean atmosphere and brilliant sunshine...and the cows seem to thrive on the salty fodder.

Extreme temperatures are unkown here and records of significative snowfalls must be sought in the archives. In summer, the average temperature is 25ºC and in winter 12ºC and this temperate climate is an added attraction for the considerable number of retired people, British in the main, who choose Menorca as their residence.

Flora and fauna

We have already mentioned the almost total absence of deciduous trees on the island. This is another consequence of the shortage of water which, in this instance, favours the growth of the evergreen varieties. Among these, the most common species are the carob, the almond, the fig and the wild olive, genetic predecessor of the olive tree. The prickly pear also abounds and is known to the Menorcans as the *figuera de moro* or Moor's fig. For use as building material or firewood, the well-established wild olive or evergreen oak are used and, to a lesser extent, the two varieties of pine that are found in the central and northern woodlands, and the sabines that grow close to the beaches and marshlands.

Other types of vegetation include the mastic bush, buckthorn, madronas, heather, myrtles, broom, oleander, bramble, juniper and wild asparagus. A multitude of wild flowers exist on the island: asphodels and orquids, gladioli, poppies and convolvulus.

Many species of small wild animals, reptiles, insects and birds are to be seen all over the island: martens, ferrets, weasels, rabbits, bats, field mice, hedgehogs, lizards and Mediterranean tortoises being the most common. There are also a few non-poisonous snakes. The fact that pairs of majestic red kites, and other birds of prey, are still a relatively frequent sight says much for the state of Menorca's wildlife, as their presence indicates the survival of many lesser species that form the lower echelons of the ecological pyramid.

Pig's ear (Dracunculus musciborus)

Suwfly orchid (Ophrys tenthredinifera)

Mediterranean tortoise.

Common egret (Egretta garzetta)

Each of the different topographic areas of the island is host to many species of birds. In the gorges: turtledoves, wood pigeons and blackbirds. On the cliffsides and harbours: seagulls, storm petrel, shearwaters and cormorants. In the woods and on cultivated land: woodcocks, goldcrests, nightjars, flycatchers, partridges and quail. In more open spaces: larks, Thikla larks, corn bunting, hoopoes and crows. During the winter, robins and orphean warblers are to be seen, along with great flocks of thrush and starlings that stop here on their way south and, during the summer, swallows, swifts, crag martins and bee-eaters arrive from North Africa.

Some parts of the island play such an important role in the migrative and reproductive cycles of these species that development projects in the vicinity have been prohibited. In the Albufera d'Es Grau where, apart from an important resident colony, thousands of birds gather each year to breed, planning permission for an urbanization was withdrawn even after building had been started. As a result, the Albufera is an ornithologist's paradise where mallards, coots, water rails, aquatic warblers, grebes, egrets, pochards and stone curlews can all be observed undisturbed in their natural habitat.

Various predatory and scavenger species can be observed all year round, although man's invasion of their nesting areas has led to the drastic reduction in the number of these larger birds. This is the case of the osprey, the booted eagle and even the red kite, but falcons, kestrels, hawks, Egyptian vultures, buzzards, marsh harriers and owls are still plentiful along with many types of small, insectivorous birds.

The sea and its riches

As befits an island, the enjoyment and appreciation of nature extends beyond the confines of the coastline to the surrounding sea where another, constantly changing panorama awaits us. The visitor who attempts to follow the perimeter of the island by land will find it a difficult task. The **Consell Insular** has started work on the restoration of the *Camí de Cavalls*, the bridle path dat-

Another bird of prey, the buzzard (Buteo buteo)

Impressive aspect of the Egyptian vulture (Neophron percnopterus)

Lizards

THE MANY SUBSPECIES OF LIZARDS TO BE FOUND ON THE ISLETS AROUND MENORCA ARE SUBJECT OF INVESTIGATION BY BIOLOGISTS AND NATURALISTS. THE FACT THAT THEY ARE BLACK HAS CREATED A DEMAND FOR THEM AS CURIOSITIES EVEN THOUGH, IT IS SAID, THEY CHANGE COLOUR ONCE REMOVED FROM THEIR NATURAL HABITAT. OVER THE YEARS, THE NUMBER OF SPECIMENS TO BE FOUND ON THE ILLA DES SARGANTANES, ILLA D'EN COLOM, AND PARTICULARLY ILLA DEL AIRE, HAS DROPPED ALARMINGLY. NOW THEY HAVE BEEN DECLARED A PROTECTED SPECIES AND LAWS HAVE BEEN PASSED TO ENSURE THAT, IN FUTURE, THOSE WHO WISH TO CONTEMPLATE THEM MUST DO SO IN SITU.

Brown cows, black horses

THE VISITOR WHO HAS SEEN THE HERDS OF BLACK AND WHITE FRIESIANS THAT ABOUND ALL OVER THE MENORCAN COUNTRYSIDE MAY BE SURPRISED BY THIS HEADING. IT IS, INDEED, RARE TO COME ACROSS EXAMPLES OF THE ISLAND'S NATIVE BREED OF HANDSOME, REDDISH-BROWN CATTLE, BUT ATTEMPTS ARE BEING MADE TO REVIVE INTEREST IN THEIR BREEDING AND, HOPEFULLY, THEIR PRESENCE WILL INCREASE IN THE NEAR FUTURE.

THERE IS, HOWEVER, NO ROOM FOR DOUBT AS REGARDS THE COLOUR OF MENORCA'S INDIGENOUS BREED OF HORSES. IN ALL THE LOCAL FESTES AND FESTIVITIES THE MAGNIFICENT JET BLACK HORSES PLAY A LEADING ROLE. THEIR MAINS AND TAILS ADORNED WITH COLOURED RIBBONS, THEY ARE THE CENTRE OF ATTRACTION AS, INDEED, ARE THE SKILLFUL JOCKEYS WHO RIDE THEM.

ing from 1682 that encircles the entire island and was used for both civil and military purposes until the middle of this century. When it is completed, walkers, cyclists and horse-riders will be able to enjoy parts of the coastline only visible at the moment from the air or the sea.

The custom of sailing round the island with overnight stops on the way, always a tradition among Menorcan families, many of whom posess recreational craft for this purpose, has also become popular with the visiting tourists. At the height of the season, the many boats to be seen in the coastal waters form a heterogeneous procession in which all sizes, styles and degrees of luxury have their place.

Those visitors who do not have the opportunity to see the island by boat can console themselves relaxing on any of the magnificent beaches which also offer the possibility of contemplating the marine floor and its fauna. Diving enthusiasts can choose between rocky and sandy sea beds; the depths that are host to grouper and scorpion fish, and the carpet of posidonia, reservoir of life and breeding ground to many crustaceans and other species. This submarine meadow, of great oxygen-generating potential, is another symbol of conservationism and must be protected against mankind, its greatest pillager.

Although many varieties of sea urchins, moluscs and crustaceans are still to be found, along with fish such as the wrasse, dentex, salema, saddled bream and combers, both the monk seal and the sea turtle have been irradicated from these waters by excessive and indiscriminate fishing which has upset the delicate ecological balance in detriment of these species.

Cala Mitjaneta

History and sociology

Since time immemorial, Menorca has suffered the logical transformations of a conquered land: many peoples and cultures have succeeded one another in occupation, imposing their customs and leaving their indelible mark. Their many and varied influences coexist here, forming the interesting mosaic that is Menorca today, enriched by centuries of change and adaption.

Peoples of the mainland of Spain and the eastern Mediterranean had settled here long before the Phoenicians, possibly as early as 4000 BC. Traces of their cultures are still apparent today in the many prehistoric monuments scattered over the island. In fact, Menorca can boast of having the greatest concentration of them in the world. After centuries of neglect, much of this unique archaelogical treasure has now been restored, and excavation work still in progress continually adds new discoveries. Recently, in a cave in the Ciutadella area, both human remains and others belonging to the *myotragus balearicus* (an extinct breed of goat) have been found along with bronze, ceramic and wooden objects, all in an excellent state of conservation.

The first recorded visitors were of a peaceable nature, first Phoenician and then Greek sailors seeking to expand their commercial activities across the Mediterranean. The Carthaginians, on the other hand, landed here with very different intentions. Lead by Magón, Hannibal's brother, they forcefully recruited the legendary *honderos*, slingshooters whose skill was to bring them fame in the Punic Wars.

The Greek name of Meloussa was changed to Minorica by the Romans when they conquered the island under Quintus Caecilius Metellus in 123 BC. They built roads and reinforced the settlements of Iammona (Ciutadella), Mago (Maó) and Sanisera (Sa Nitja), established by the

Carthaginians at a time when the Insulae Balearis was a newly created Roman province in its own right, previously having formed part of the province of Tarragona. Much has still to be discovered about the Roman occupation of the island as has become apparent following the new excavations being carried out in the port of Sanitja. Some of the findings are on show in the Ecomuseu de Cap de Cavalleria (see p.119). It appears that the natives of the island lived in harmony with the new occupiers until the 5th century AD and the arrival of the Vandals which gave rise to cruel persecution of the Christians.

For some time now, Christianity had become firmly established on the island. Bishop Severo's famous epistle of the year 417, describes travelling from Mago to Iammona with the aim of converting the city's Jewish colony. In 533, the Byzantines overthrew the Vandals, Christianity was restored and there follows a period about which comparatively little is known.

In the year 903, Menorca fell to the Moors. Under the ñew name of Minurka, the island was divided into four districts, the capital was established in Ciutadella (Medina Minurka) and the fort was built on Sta. Àgueda (Sen Agaiz). The majority of the populace was disseminated over the island and lived off the land which, thanks to the techniques of irrigation farming introduced by the Moors, became more fertile and productive and trading routes were established with Italian ports. Although few monuments dating from this time remain, the Moorish influence is ever-present today in many of the island's place names, for example, those starting with Bini which, in the language of the Moors meant "son or heir of".

⊖⊖ *Bronze statue of the Imhotep, a healing god. Found at the Torre d'en Gaumés site, it supposedly dates from the later Talayotic period.*

⊖⊖ *Roman coin, with the value of a silver denarius, representing the goddess Roma. It dates from 146 BC and was found at the Sanisera excavation. Today it can be seen in the Ecomuseu de Cap de Cavalleria.*

⊖⊖ *Small, bronze image of a bull, found at the Torralba d'en Salord taula. Probably a votive element, it dates from the 3rd or 4th century BC.*

⊘ *Punic amphora from Binicalaf, typical of the 2nd century BC when the eastern Mediterranean's commercial activity was based in Eivissa.*

⊘ *Pre-Talayotic funerary piece dated circa 1800-2000 BC. Found near Alaior, it now forms part of the Vives Escudero collection.*

⊘ *Reconstruction of a ceramic urn from the late Talayotic era. The remains were found at the Trepucó site.*

The Catalan conquest

In the 13th century, the Balearics, along with the rest of the Iberian peninsula, were recaptured from the Moors for Christianity. Mallorca was taken by Jaume I of Aragón and in 1232 Menorca declared feudal allegiance to him which was maintained until 1287 when the island was conquered by a confederate army led by Alfons III. The Moors were taken as slaves or sent home in return for ransom. Of the latter, many never arrived but were thrown overboard shortly after setting sail. Alfons III shared the reconquered land as booty among his knights and this led to a certain deterioration of the island's social and economic structure.

After a brief period of progress and improvement, and until the end of the Middle Ages, the history of Menorca can be summarised as a time of epidemics, poverty, decadence and confrontation between the ruling classes and the peasantry. Following this, the 16th century can only be described in even worse terms, as, during the negligent reigns of Carlos I and Felipe II, many tragedies took place. In 1535 a fleet led by the cruel Turk Barbarossa admiral of Sultan Solimán II, sacked the city of Maó, razed it to the ground and imprisoned the populace. In 1558, the Turks attacked Ciutadella with similar consequences. More than three thousand people were taken as slaves to Constantinople, and the city's heritage of historical documents was destroyed.

The 17th century was as ill-fated as its predecessors. Epidemics of bubonic plague, the constant threat of pirate raids and the destruction of crops by swarms of locusts further undermined the peasantry while the nobility and the clergy grew stronger in the face of these adversities. The events of the 18th century and the change of sovereignty they brought were, therefore, beneficial. The century began with confrontations between followers of the Archduke of Austria, pretender to the Spanish throne, and those of Felipe de Borbón. The outbreak of the War of Succession in 1706 plunged the island into a state of civil war. France sent troops to support the Borbón cause, thus enabling Anglo-Dutch forces to disembark and take the island with hardly a shot fired. In 1712, the Treaty of Utrecht ceded the island of Menorca to the British Crown.

British and French domination

The British domination that lasted from 1708 to 1756 has been described by historians as the Golden Age of Menorca. If injusticies were committed by some members of the governing body, they were rapidly rectified and Richard Kane, the first Governor, is remembered with praise. He introduced fodder farming, imported fresh breeding stock, built the road across the island that still bears his name, abolished the Inquisition, and built schools. Under his rule, only the interests of Ciutadella can said to have been prejudiced. The British, Protestant domination was not well accepted here by the nobility and clergy and, as a result, the city lost its status as capital in favour of Maó which benefitted greatly from the consequent increase in commercial activity.

In 1756, the Duke of Richelieu, with a contingent of twenty thousand French troops, disembarked in Ciutadella where they were well received by the devoutly Catholic population. After a brief naval skirmish, the British withdrew with full military honours although Admiral Byng returned to England in disgrace where he was subsequently court-martialled and executed. For the next seven years, Menorca was ruled by the French. During this time, the Governor, Conde de Lannion, reinstated some of Ciutadella's lost status, founded the village of St. Lluís in honour of King Louis... and Richelieu discovered mayonnaise which was a great success at the court of Versailles. At the end of the Seven Years War in 1763, The Treaty of Paris returned Menorca to the British Crown.

During this second domination, the British were not as benevolent as they had been in the past, and the only notable work carried out by them was the demolition of the *arraval* of St. Felip and the transfer of its inhabitants to Georgetown, known today as Es Castell. A number of Menorcans, owing to the conditions of extreme poverty that now prevailed, emigrated to Florida in search of better fortune and others became privateers. After nineteen years of bad government and injustice, in 1782, a Franco-Spanish fleet, under Duque de Crillon, reconquered the island for Carlos III of Spain after a six month siege.

In 1798 the British returned for the last time, staying until 1802 when Menorca was finally returned to the

⊕⊕ *This Gothic inscription, commemorating the conquest of the island by Alfons III, once decorated the Pont de na Gentil bridge in Maó.*

⊕ *These oil paintings on canvas have been attributed, for the similarity in style and content, to the landscapist Joan Font i Vidal (1811-1855), although only the one in the centre, dated "10th October 1850", bears his signature.*

Spanish Crown after seventy-two years of foreign occupation. Despite the good government of Conde de Cifuentes, Carlos III's representative on the island, the Spanish administration brought with it the seal of totalitarianism with a consequent loss of civil liberties, and, during the reigns of Carlos IV and Fernando VII, decadence and corruption prevailed throughout society. Once again, emigration was the only solution for many Menorcans who now ventured to Algiers and other north-African cities. Not until the middle of the 19th century did industrialization permit a relative economic recovery.

Recent history

This industrialization brought with it the beginnings of labour movements which, in turn, instigated many social changes. For example, a general strike was held in protest against the war in Morocco and the workers of the shoemaking industry formed an Anarquist federation. The collapse of the First Republic and the return of the Monarchy, supported by the landowning aristocracy, strengthened the position of the old ruling classes. The parliamentary elections of 1879 were won by the Conservatives in the Balearics, their member for Menorca being the Duque de Almenara Alta.

With the ascension to the throne of Alfonso XIII in 1902, the whole Spanish political system entered into a period of crisis and both Liberals and Conservatives failed in their attempts at innovation. In Menorca, only the Conservatives carried any weight within Monarchist circles, but the Republican party was strongly supported and in several legislations represented the island at Parliament. Proof of the Menorcans' truly democratic disposition at that time can be found in their lack of support for neither the candidatures presented by Joan March in Mallorca and Pere Matutes in Eivissa (which could be described as despotic or totalitarian by nature), nor the reactionary dictatorship of Primo de Rivera. At the local elections of 1931, whose results led to the proclamation of the Second Republic, the seat for Menorca was won by the *Front Únic* formed by Socialists and Republicans.

Following the Nationalist insurrection that gave rise to the outbreak of the Spanish Civil War, the military commander declared the island's allegiance to the Francoist rebellion. However, the very next day, 20th July 1936, a combined force of civilians and noncommissioned officers rose against the insurgent armed forces and, at the cost of great loss of

life, won Menorca back for the Republic. The island resisted until the end of the war in February 1939 and was, in fact, the last position in Spain to fall to the Nationalist troops. The bloody reprisals perpetrated in retaliation form one of the most traumatic chapters of Menorcan history.

The social and economic consequences of nearly forty years of dictatorship are too far-reaching and complex to be dealt with here in detail. The one-party system, strengthened by a powerful bureaucracy, generated political apathy among the popu-

⟰ Anonymous painting, dated 1835, in which the activities of Maó harbour are illustrated in great detail. The warehouses in the foreground stand at the foot of the hill that connected the quayside with what is now the Miranda Square. Social classes such as merchants and clergy are represented, as are the different trades of the time: boatbuilders, peasants, fishermen, stevedores, gin distillers, etc.

⟲ Oil painting on canvas, dated and signed B. Pax 1859, showing the Industrial Mahonesa factory, opened in 1856 in Cala Figuera.

lace and, until the 1950s, there was no apparent sign of unrest at any social level. The latter end of the 1960s, a time of prosperity for the island, witnessed the first, albeit clandestine, indications of a desire for the revival of democracy. They were to remain repressed until the 1970s and the flood of events that changed the course of Spanish history: the death of the dictator and restoration of the monarchy in King Juan Carlos I (November 1975), the reform process that led to the first democratic elections since the Second Republic (June 1977), and the enactment by the King of the new Constitution (December 1978).

More recently, in 1982, Parliament accepted the *Estatut d' Autonomía de les Illes Balears* which allows a degree of home rule for the islands under the *Consells Insulars*, or island councils.

Economy

The basis of the island's current economic profile must be sought in the first shoe factories that were set up in Ciutadella around the year 1850. The industrialization of the industry marked the start of an era in which Menorcan produce was successfully promoted abroad. Commerce with both the continent and the Spanish colonies brought notable progress and prosperity to the island and gave rise to the creation of other subsidiary activities.

In 1856 the Industrial Mahonesa opened the island's pioneer textile and cotton-spinning factory in the port of Maó (where the CAMPSA depot is now) and the following years were a time of prosperity during which many businesses and industries were set up. The loss of the Cuban market in 1898 plunged the shoemaking industry into a severe recession which lasted until the First World War. At the same time, however, by 1911 three thousand people were employed in the manufacture of silver purses, an activity considered to be the precursor of the present-day costume-jewellery industry.

After 1870, the extensive cultivation of cattle fodder converted dairy farming into the principal agricultural activity with the consequent increase in meat and milk production, the latter being made into cheese.

Tourism, as an industry, arrived in Menorca between the end of the 1950s and the beginning of the 1960s, but its advance was far slower than in Mallorca or Eivissa due to the fact that, here, it was considered an alternative source of income rather

Footwear and *Avarques*

A CENSUS CARRIED OUT IN 1782 (WHEN MENORCA WAS ONCE AGAIN UNDER SPANISH RULE) INDICATED THAT 281 ISLANDERS WERE SHOEMAKERS BY TRADE. THEIR CUSTOMERS WERE MEMBERS OF THE ARISTOCRACY AND MILITARY OFFICERS, AND THE FIRST STEPS WERE BEING TAKEN TO ESTABLISH AN EXPORT TRADE. SINCE THOSE DAYS, THIS INDUSTRY HAS KNOWN TIMES OF GREAT PROSPERITY BUT ALSO IMPORTANT SETBACKS AND RECESSIONS SUCH AS THE LOSS OF THE CUBAN MARKET AT THE TURN OF THE CENTURY. THANKS TO THE SKILL AND PROFESSIONALITY OF THE CRAFTSMEN OF ALAIOR AND CIUTADELLA, THE PRESTIGE OF MENORCAN FOOTWEAR PREVAILS TODAY. AS COMPETITION ITENSIFIED FROM OTHER SOURCES WITH LOWER PRODUCTION COSTS, THE INDUSTRY HERE WAS OBLIGED TO MOVE UP INTO THE MARKET OF FASHION-DESIGN. NEVERTHELESS, ONE OF THE MOST SUCCESSFUL LINES ARE THE PEASANT SANDALS OR *AVARQUES*, COMPRISED OF TWO PIECES OF COWHIDE ATTACHED TO A PNEUMATIC SOLE, WORN HERE SINCE TIME IMMEMORIAL. THEY ARE NOW PRODUCED IN MORE SOPHISTICATED VERSIONS AND ARE SUCH AN INTRINSIC SYMBOL OF MENORCA THAT MINIATURE CHINA COPIES ARE SOLD AS SOUVENIRS.

than the mainstay of the economy. Even so, by 1973 it was important enough to be considered as one of the three chief economic supports, the others being arable and dairy farming, and the costume-jewellery and shoemaking industries.

This balance has been upset by a series of events, such as Spain's entry into the E.C. in 1986 which has severely affected the dairy farming industry, and the strong competition presented to the costume-jewellery and footwear sectors by Asian manufacturers whose labour and raw material costs cannot be rivalled here. Isolation, such an inherent part of Menorca's character, pays a high price in terms of commercial viability, and it is yet to be seen how the island's industries will deal with the challenges to be faced in the near future.

Prehistoric monuments

Although an exhaustive discovery of the island's archaeological treasures may well be beyond the possibilities of the average visitor, the Southeastern Area car tour, see page 116, and the indications at the end of the Around Ciutadella tour, page 114, suffice as an introduction to this subject, one of Menorca's most fascinating themes.

The oldest remains (megalithic tombs, underground caves and *navetas*) have been dated by experts at around 2000 BC, but the most notable examples date from what is known as the *talaiotic* era, from around 1400 BC to the Roman invasion of the island in the last century BC. During this time, the structural conception, and even some of the materials used, changed considerably, to a certain extent as a result of increased contact with the outside world. Successive stages of this process are quite patent in some cases, the last recognizable influence being Punic, coinciding with the foundation of Mago, Iammona and Sanisera. These settlements were still inhabited by the native population during the Roman occupation.

The monuments that date from the talaiotic era are easily recognizable and are classified as: burial caves, burial chambers, *talaiots*, walled enclosures and *taules*.

Prehistoric settlement at Talatí de Dalt

Monuments from other historical periods to be found on the island are the early-Christian basilicas built during the 5th and 6th centuries during occupation by the Vandals and, supposedly, the Byzantines. The most famous is at **Son Bou**, where its proximity to the waterline has given rise to speculation about the possible existence of other nearby buildings. Indeed, some curious structures (visible from the air) do exist on the sea-bed just off-shore from the basilica, and their apparently regular shapes suggest the remains of a settlement. Archaeologists are, however, sceptic on this point. Inside the basilica, a baptismal font, carved from a single stone, is of particular interest. At **Es Fornàs**, near St. Climent, there is another basilica dated 6th century BC where we can see a superb mosaic of animal and vegetable motifs, and another on the **Illa del Rei** whose mosaics have been moved to the **Museu de Menorca**.
At **Cap d'es Port de Fornells** and on the **Illa d'en Colom**, two more are to be found, the latter currently undergoing excavation work.

Caves at Cales Coves

Burial caves

The most interesting of their kind are to be found at **Cales Coves**, on the south coast a few kilometres from Sant Climent, where nearly one hundred appear on the cliff face. There are more at **Caparrot de Forma** (near Es Canutells), at **Son Bou** (beneath a fortified wall on the cliff) and at **Cala Morell** on the north coast. All these burial sites date from the 9th and 8th centuries BC, but seem to have been in use well into the Roman era.

Burial *navetes*

The name *naveta* (little boat) is derived from their appearance, resembling that of an inverted hull. The oldest, dating from pre-talaiotic times, are oval or circular in shape, but their construction evolved towards more elongated forms, for example, the **Naveta d'Es Tudons** of circa 1400 BC. A tiny doorway gives access to the interior which is comprised of an anteroom or entrance hall and one or two superimposed chambers. These constructions, of purely funerary use, are the oldest in Europe of their kind and can be found at **Biniac, Llumena, Rafal Rubí** and **Son Morell**.

Naveta des Tudons near Ciutadella

Torelló talaiot

Talaiots

Talaiots are situated on rises in the ground or hillocks, from where other *talaiots* are usually visible at a distance. This fact has led to the supposition that they were used as defence towers or lookout points (*talaies* in Catalan) hence their name. However, remains have been found in small chambers inside these truncated cones which suggest that they were used as burial places. These great mounds of stone, up to ten metres tall, are to be found all over the island in varying stages of conservation.
The most notable stand at: **Trepucó, Torre Trencada, Talatí de Dalt, Torre Llafuda, Torre Llisà Nou, Torre d'en Gaumés** and **Binimaimut**.

Taules

These are the most exceptional of all the talaiotic monuments and are unique to Menorca, whereas constructions similar to *talaiots* are to be found elsewhere. They comprise of two huge blocks of limestone and owe their name *taules* (tables in Catalan) to their T-shaped form. Their most notable characteristic is their size: the *taula* at **Torralba d'en Salord**, which is imbedded two metres in the ground, weighs approximately 25 tons.

They are surrounded by a series of niches in the shape of a horse-shoe which were probably used for depositing offerings to the deity.
Opinions vary as to the purpose of the *taules*: sacrificial altar, central supporting pillar of a roof, symbol of a deity, or a fertility symbol in the form of the head and horns of a bull...
The most important are at: **Trepucó, Torre Trencada, Talatí de Dalt, Torre Llafuda, Torre Llisà Vell, Torre d'en Gaumés** and **Binimaimut**.

Taula de Talati

Rural architecture

The rural arquitecture of Menorca, so different from that of Mallorca, Eivissa or other parts of the Mediterranean, forms an integral part of the landscape and, as such, has a significance that rises above and beyond merely practical considerations.

The whiteness of the farmhouses and hamlets scattered across the countryside is one of the island's most characteristic images. The task of whitewashing is an activity in which the islanders, usually the women, invest a great deal of time and energy, taking logical pride in the immaculate results they achieve. Their motives are not only aesthetic, however, as the frequent painting not only assures the cleanliness, but also the protection of the limestone walls that would otherwise be eaten away by sun, rain and wind. This stone, and *ullastre*, the wood from the wild olive tree, were the only raw building materials to be found on the island. Easily cut into ashlars, or building blocks, *marès* was readily available, either at the building site itself, or from any of the many quarries.

The basic configuration of Menorcan rural arquitecture was determined by the limited range of available raw materials and the prevailing climate. Houses were always built facing south, with a minimum of doors and windows on the north side to exclude the cold *tramuntana* wind. The sun heats the porches during the winter months and rainwater is collected by a curious system of gutters made from Moorish-style roof tiles that canalize it down from the roof to the cistern or water tank. All these elements make of the Menorcan farmhouse a clear example of man's adjustment to the means at his disposal.

Details of typical architecture

Another characteristic of the countryside are the endless dry- stone walls that, when seen from the air, appear as an enormous crisscross network. Their purpose is to divide up the *llocs* or farm-steads into individual *tanques* or fields for rotation farming. At the same time, their construction cleared the fields of stones and prevents the sparse topsoil from being blown away by the strong winds. Some of these stones were used to construct protective walls around tree trunks. True craftsmen, the few remaining *paredadors* still work in the same ancestral way building a double wall which is then filled in with rubble. To make them easier to climb, a few stones are left protruding up both side to form rudimentary steps known as *botadors*. The wooden gates, often made of twisted *acebuche*, another example of local craftsmanship, prevent cattle and sheep from straying and should always be left as they are found.

Marès was the only available building material in times gone by

Quarries

THE ASSOCIATION BETWEEN MENORCA AND STONE, WHETHER IN ITS NATURAL STATE OR MANIPULATED BY MAN, IS INEVITABLE. WHEN BUILDING STYLES MOVED AWAY FROM THE USE OF RUDIMENTARY, CRUDE STONE TOWARDS THE USE OF LIMESTONE ASHLARS, THESE WERE INVARIABLY OBTAINED FROM THE SITES THEMSELVES. LATER, THE INCREASING DEMAND GAVE RISE TO THE CONSTRUCTION OF QUARRIES WHERE THOUSANDS OF TONS OF RAW MATERIAL WAS HEWED, BY HAND, IN REGULAR SHAPED BLOCKS. TIMES HAVE CHANGED, AND THE INTRODUCTION OF NEW ELEMENTS HAS CAUSED THE QUARRIES TO FALL INTO DISUSE.

NO LONGER EXPLOITED, THEY SEEM DESTINED TO REMAIN AS SCARS UPON THE LANDSCAPE, BUT **LÍTHICA**, A RECENTLY FORMED ASSOCIATION, HAS PLANS TO SAVE THEM FROM SUCH AN IGNOMINIOUS FATE AND REFURBISH THEM FOR VARIOUS CULTURAL ACTIVITIES.

Fêtes and festes

Throughout the summer, each town celebrates in turn its own local *festes*, during which the islanders have always given rein to their ancestral love of merriment. Today they are enthusiastically joined by the many summer visitors and the first and most famous of these events is held in Ciutadella in honour of St. John the Baptist. These are the first *festes* of the season, and the cycle is closed by those of Maó on the 7th and 8th September. The *Festes de Sant Joan* begin on the Sunday prior to June 24th, when a man dressed in animal skins carries a sheep through the streets of the city, and reach their climax on the night of the 23rd and the 24th, St. John's day. At all times during the celebrations, the horse is the ever-present centre of attraction. The official acts are based on medievel traditions, and the strict observation of protocol is safeguarded by the *Junta de Caixers*, or committee, which represents the different historical social classes, peasantry, nobility and clergy all of which are symbolically rep-

resented in the processions. The *Festes de Sant Joan* are, without doubt, among the most colourful and exuberant to be held anywhere in Spain. No visitor should miss this remarkable medieval spectacle of jousting, tournaments and cavalcades, unique example of ancestral traditions and Mediterranean joie-de-vivre.

◑◑ *Jaleo in the Plaça des Born in Ciutadella. Popular folk group, adornments on a horse's tail, and detail of adornment Be de St. Joan.*

◑ *Engravings showing two of the symbols of Sant Joan.*

ES CAIXER FADRI

S'HOMO DES BE

Maó

The façades of many buildings in Maó are again being painted the pale sienna colour that had been customary until, in an attempt to live up to the slogan "Menorca, the blue and white island", an over-zealous mayor ordered them all to be whitewashed. Much restoration and conservation has been carried out, not only by the municipal authorities, but also by private individuals who take pride in maintaining, for example, the English-style sash windows of their homes. In the early morning, before the first onslaught of traffic, it is easy to imagine the aspect the town presented at the height of its prosperity in the 18th century, and the liberal and cultured society that developed here.

Clustered high on the cliff, the old part of the city overlooks the harbour. The views from the stately houses on Carrer Isabel II are particularly splendid as befits their opulent interiors and the ample proportions of their frontages.
At one end of this street, the **cloister of St. Francesc**, the first convent built in Maó in 1719, is undergoing exhaustive renovation and will eventually house the archaelogical treasures of the **Museu de Menorca** where they will be exhibited in surroundings worthy of their historical value. At the opposite end of Isabel II in Pla de la Parròquia (or Pl. Sta. Maria) we find the church of the same name, the neo-classical **Town Hall**, the clock given to the city by Governor Kane, and the building known as **Principal de Guàrdia**. The Town Hall houses a collection of portraits of famous historical figures, notably that of Conde de Lannion by Giuseppe Chiesa and Conde de Cifuentes by Pascual Calbó.

View of the harbour

Market, Claustre del Carme

The **church of Sta. Maria** is home to one of the city's treasures: the magnificent organ of 3210 pipes, 51 stops and 4 keyboards built by the German maestros Otter and Kirburz. The quality of its register delights those who attend the concerts given regularly by internationally renowned musicians who consider it a privilege to perform here. Behind Sta. Maria, built in the reign of Alfons III, a statue of this king stands in the centre of the Pl. de la Conquesta, also site of the Can Mercadal palace and the public library. From one corner of the square it is a short walk to the viewpoint which overlooks the **Costa de Ses Voltes**, a landscaped stairway leading down to the port, one of the key images first perceived by visitors arriving by boat. At its foot, the area of the port known as **Baixamar**, which in recent years has become a nucleus of bars and restaurants and centre of the city's nightlife, particularly in the summer.

Traces of the commercial activity that used to be the main characteristic of the harbour can still be found in the remaining old buildings, once the workshops of the *mestres d'aixa*, or artisan boat-builders. (In some, one can still see enormous rafters made from the salvaged masts of wooden

ships). Their skills are still renowned today and can be appreciated in the custom-built *llaüts*. These vessels are no longer used solely as fishing boats, but have become the ideal recreational craft for the many people who explore the island's coastline during the summer months. Indeed, the whole aspect of the harbour has changed as a result of the growing popularity of nautical sports, one more aspect of the influence of tourism. Nowadays, hardly anyone remembers when merchant ships docked here to unload grain for grinding in Menorcan mills, en route to their final destination on the mainland of Spain. Today, the craft found alongside the

Maó cheese

EVEN THOUGH IT IS PRODUCED ALL OVER THE ISLAND, MENORCAN CHEESE IS REFERRED TO AS *MAÓ* AS ITS COMMERCIALIZATION HAS ALWAYS BEEN BASED IN THE CAPITAL. IT IS ALSO CALLED THUS UNDER THE DENOMINATION OF ORIGIN, CONCEEDED IN 1985. SINCE THE 1960'S, THE CHEESE PRODUCED ON THE ISLAND CAN BE CALCULATED IN MILLIONS OF KILOS PER YEAR. ITS QUALITY WAS ALREADY BEING PRAISED IN MEDIEVAL CHRONICLES THAT TELL OF THE PREDILECTION OF THE CATALAN KINGS FOR THIS VARIETY

IT IS A SEMI-FAT CHEESE, MADE FROM FULL COW'S MILK TO WHICH A MAXIMUM PERMITTED 5% OF EWE'S MILK MAY BE ADDED. THE CHEESES ARE SQUARE IN SHAPE WITH ROUNDED EDGES AND, WHEN HANDMADE IN THE TRADITIONAL WAY, BEAR CHARACTERISTIC MARKS CAUSED BY THE WHITE LINEN CLOTH IN WHICH THE MILK, ONCE CURDLED, IS WRAPPED. THE WHEY IS DRAINED OUT MANUALLY AND THE BUNDLE LEFT UNDER WEIGHTS FOR TWENTY-FOUR HOURS. THEN IT IS SUBMERGED IN SALT WATER FOR TWO DAYS BEFORE THE DRYING PROCESS IS STARTED. ACCORDING TO THE DEGREE OF MATURITY, IT IS SOLD AS *TENDRE* (YOUNG), *SEMICURAT* (SEMIMATURE), *CURAT* (MATURE) OR *VELL* (VERY MATURE).

Maó from the harbour.

Club Marítim are modern, luxurious yachts, and more facilities for mooring and wintering are planned for the future.

But let's return to the starting point of our descent down to the waterfront - the **Costa de Ses Voltes**. This is where the fish market is to be found and, a little further on, the meat, fruit and vegetable market, situated in what was once the cloister and ground floor cells of the convent adjoined to the **Carme church**. The market itself is well worth visiting for the originality of its setting and it is also a short cut through to **Plaça Miranda**, another excellent viewpoint over the harbour. From here, via Plaça del Príncep, we return to the pedestrian zone of **S'Arravaleta** and **Carrer Nou**. This is the commercial centre of the town and the number and nature of passers-by are an indication, in summer, of the success of the tourist season, and in winter a mirror of Menorcan society.

The Cuesta Deià leads up to the **Teatre Principal**, inaugurated as an opera-house in 1829 and, as such, older than the Liceu of Barcelona, to which it had been compared in style until the Liceu was destroyed by fire in January 1994. The interior of the building is well-worth a visit, and this will again be possible when current refurbishment is completed.

Each spring, an opera week is held here to the satisfaction of Maó's notoriously music-loving inhabitants. The Montcada house on the corner of Carrer Bastion and Carrer Hannover has a striking modernist *uindou* (the name is a local evolution of the English window, an element often adopted here instead of typically Mediterranean balconies for climatic reasons. Further along, we reencounter the remains of the medieval city walls, the **Arc de Sant**

Modernist window

Roc which leads to S'Arraval, the dividing line between what was once the fortified city and the suburbs.

Another important central street is Dr. Orfila (or **Carrer de ses Moreres**), into which both Carrer Cifuentes and Cós de Gràcia converge from opposite sides. Following Es Cós, we arrive at the cemetery and **shrine of Our Lady of Grace**, patron saint of the city. The old orthodox temple of St. Nicolau stands on the corner of Carrer Ramon y Cajal which leads, in turn, to the **Es Freginal park**, once a place of communal market-gardening. The **scientific and literary Athenaeum**, home of an important collection of fossiles and algae and site of many cultural activities, stands of Carrer Conde de Cifuentes and, behind it, **S'Esplanada**, the main square of the city.

Bordered by the barracks built during the first British domination, the construction in recent years of an underground car park has altered, yet again, the configuration of the old parade ground. Here people of all ages gather to pass the time of day and a street market is held twice a week. Its also the point of departure of the main roads that lead to other parts of the island and site of the bus terminus. Currently, it is rumoured that the remaining barracks are to be moved to another location. This would be a positive step in the Esplanada's evolution from military to civic centre.

Es Castell

The name of this town has been changed many times during the course of its history: Arraval de St. Felip, Georgetown, in honour of King George III during the British occupation, Villacarlos after King Carlos III of Spain and, finally, **Es Castell** which has recently become the official name and refers to the Castle of St. Felip which stood here from 1554 until its demolition in 1781. Military history has played a vital role in the town throughout the centuries, and is still apparent in the barracks that surround S'Esplanada, the main square, alongside the colonial-style Town Hall. Inside the neo-classical church of Roser there is an interesting stone alterpiece that once belonged in the castle chapel.

Cales Fonts, down on the waterfront, was once the site of fishermens' boathouses but, over the years, has been transformed into lively centre of bars and restaurants. From here, sightseeing trips by boat can be taken around Maó harbour and over to **Lazareto**. This fortified precint only became an island in 1900 when the Alfons XII canal was constructed, and it served as a quarantine centre in the 18th and 19th centuries. Today it is used as a congress centre and holiday accommodation for Ministry of Health employees. There is a small museum of medical instruments and other curiosities in one of the buildings.

Sant Lluís

St. Lluís was founded at the end of the 18th century during the French occupation. They layout of its streets was planned by Conde de Lannion, as was the building of some of the outlying hamlets. In those days, their function was purely rural, but of

Cales Fonts, Es Castell

Es Molí de Dalt, ethnologic museum, Sant Lluís

Panoramic view of Fornells harbour

late they have become residential areas. However, thanks to local legislation, their original outward appearance has been conserved.

In the town itself, the major landmarks are the governor's house and the church dedicated to the patron saint, St. Louis, King of France. Several old windmills still stand, and one, the **Molí de Dalt**, situated opposite the Plaça Nova by the bus stop, has been converted into an interesting ethnological museum.

The coastline around St. Lluís abounds in coves, beaches and urbanizations: **S'Algar**, **Alcalfar**, **Punta Prima**, B**inisafúller** and **Binibèquer** all bear witness to the growth of the tourist industry.

Alaior

In 1304, King Jaume II of Mallorca founded what we know today as **Alaior** on the site of a farmstead named *Ihalor*. It is sometimes called the island's third capital on account of its historical role as mediator between Maó and Ciutadella and the independence afforded it by a balanced economy based on farming, tourism and light industry. **Son Bou, San Jaime** and **Cala en Porter** are the main tourist centres of the area. The most notable buildings are **Casa Salord**, the **Town Hall** and the church of **Sta. Eulàlia** (rebuilt after damage by a tornado at the end of the 17th century). The cloister of the church of **St. Dídac**, now popularly known as *Pati de Sa Lluna*, has undergone a major transformation over

Aerial view of Alaior

the years. What were once the cells have been transformed into living accommodation by people of varied origins and life styles. Outside the town, the visitor may be surprised to see a number of houses of intriguing names and architectural styles that seem out of place in the Menorcan countryside. They were built by local people of past generations who ventured overseas during the economic recessions that afflicted the island and evoke memories of the exotic lands they visited.

Es Mercadal and Fornells

At the geographical heart of the island, at the foot of **Monte Toro**, **Es Mercadal** owes its name to the privilege bestowed by King Jaume II to Catalan colonials, authorizing them to hold a market here every Thursday of the year. This custom prevails today in a handicraft market also held on Tuesday and Saturday afternoons. This is a pictoresque little town whose old centre is crossed by a watercourse. The majority of the population is still employed on the many outlying farms. However, in neighbouring **Fornells** and the nearby urbanizations, the local economy depends almost entirely upon the tourist and service industries although development has been restricted to low-rise holiday homes and much of the atmosphere of the old

fishing village may still be enjoyed today. The island's only golf course is to be found near here at **Son Parc**.

The parish church of **St. Martí** in Es Mercadal is a renaissance building with some later additions dating from 1807. Also worth seeing is the cistern built under British patronage by Pere Carreras in 1735 that brought drinking water to the town for the first time and is named after Richard Kane, the British Governor of the time.

Home-made sweets and confectionery from **Ca's Sucrer** and *avarques*, typical Menorcan sandals from Biel **Servera's workshop** are two attractions for both visitors and locals alike. Several restaurants in

Es Mercadal from the road to Monte Toro

Rooftops of Ferreries

Es Mercadal specialise in traditional Menorcan dishes and of course **Fornells**, with its famous lobster specialities, is an indispensable port of call.

Ferreries

Ferreries exemplifies the transformation that has taken place on the island since the beginning of tourist-orientated development in the 1960's. The shoe, costume jewellery and furniture-making industries employ a sector of the population previously dedicated to agriculture, and dairy farming has taken over from arable farming as the major rural activity. Building, commerce and service industries complete the rest of the town's economic profile. Opinions are divided over the origins of the name Ferreries, some opting for the existence of a nearby monastery of friars, *fraria*, and others for the idea that it was founded by an iron-worker, *ferrer*. What is for certain is that the town was established by King Jaume II of Mallorca, in the 14th century, who built the church of **St. Bartomeu** which presides over the centre of the old town. However, the remodelled Pl. Espanya is the centre of activity today and on Saturdays hosts a handicraft market.

In the neighbouring area, places of interest include the **Algendar gorge**, **Cala Galdana** and **Mount Sta. Àgueda** (264m.) where the ruins of a Moorish fortification still stand.

Es Migjorn

Es Migjorn became a municipality in its own right in 1989, (previously it was dependant on Es Mercadal), but its origins must be sought two centuries ago during the second British occupation. Until then, the local farmers had to take their pro-

Church of Sant Cristòfol. Es Migjorn Gran

Sa Plaça Nova and Ses Voltes

The Town Hall from the port

duce to Ferreries to be sold, but the construction of the church of **St. Cristòfol** and surrounding dwellings offered them alternative trading opportunities. Here, the peace and quiet of traditional, rural Menorca is more apparent than elsewhere on the island and, even in summer, when tourists crowd the nearby beaches of **St. Adeodat** and **St. Tomàs**, Es Migjorn Gran still retains much of its intrinsic charm.

Ciutadella

Although **Ciutadella** can be likened to other cities or towns of similar evolution, a series of characteristics combine here to create a special atmosphere, an intangible difference. Its inhabitants are aware of this and maintain it with pride, as if in retaliation for the loss of their city's status as island capital. They offer visitors a generous welcome but never cease to be themselves, often emphasising these differences rather than seeking to atenuate them. In speech, as well, they use turns of phrase and expressions in Catalan that have fallen into disuse elsewhere. For these reasons, visitors already familiar with the rest of the island may feel, on arrival in **Ciutadella,** that they have entered another world.

Of the old city walls, only two bastions have survived the course of history: **Es Born** on top of which the **Town Hall** was constructed, and **Sa Font** at the point where a stream once emerged into the harbour. It is, however, easy to imagine the totality of the original form of the walls as they have been replaced by three consecutive avenues: Constitució, Jaume I, and Capità Negrete, known collectively as **Sa Contramurada**. The **Camí de Maó**, name given to the final stretch of the main road as it enters Ciutadella, leads to the Pl. Alfons III where the Porta de Maó gateway once gave access to the city. It is a typically Mediterranean square, lively with cafés and outdoor terraces, one of which occupies the recently restored **Es Compte windmill**. Continuing along the **Camí de Maó**, we arrive at **Sa Plaça Nova** and then Carrer José Mª. Quadrado, or **Ses Voltes**, one of the most characteristic streets, with its narrow pavement and vaulted arcade. Although the ground floors of the buildings that flank it are now occupied by all kinds of shops, it has not lost it charm and medieval aspect. In Sa Plaça Vella, on top of a stone column, stands one of the city's most emblematic symbols, the tiny *Be de Sant Joan* (Lamb of St. John), work of the local artist Maties Quetglas. Ses Voltes leads us to the **Sta. Maria cathedral**.

Built in Catalan Gothic style in the 14th century on the site of a Moslem mosque, **Sta. Maria** does not stand out from its surroundings in terms of height. It is however, an impressive, forceful building comprised of one sole nave that has been repaired and rebuilt so many times that elements of various architectural styles are to be found, such as the baroque **chapel of Ses Ànimes** and the neoclassical main façade. Historical events of all kinds have left their mark here, notably in 1558, the year of *sa desgràcia* (misfortune), when the cathedral was

Es Gin

ALTHOUGH ITS ORIGIN CAN BE TRACED TO THE TIMES OF THE BRITISH DOMINATION OF THE ISLAND, THIS LOCAL BREW BEARS LITTLE RESEMBLANCE TO ENGLISH GIN, BEING MORE SIMILAR TO THE DUTCH VARIETY. ONLY ONE DISTILLERY, XORIGUER, REMAINS TODAY AND IN THEIR FACTORY IN THE PORT ONE CAN SEE THE ANTIQUE STILLS WHERE THE JUNIPER BERRIES CONTINUE TO BE PROCESSED IN ACCORDANCE WITH THE TRADITIONAL RECIPE THAT DATES FROM THE 18TH CENTURY. THE CLAY BOTTLES IN WHICH GIN WAS ORIGINALLY SOLD ARE COLLECTORS' PIECES NOWADAYS, BUT XORIGUER DOES COMMERCIALIZE PART OF ITS PRODUCE IN EARTHENWARE REPLICAS. GIN IS DRUNK STRAIGHT OR IN COMBINATION WITH *HERBES*, A LIQUEUR MADE LOCALLY FROM A MIXTURE OF WILD HERBS IN WHICH CAMOMILE IS THE MOST DOMINANT; WITH A SLICE OF LEMON AND A SPLASH OF SODA-WATER, IN WHICH CASE IT IS CALLED A *PALLOFA*; OR WATERED-DOWN WITH LEMON SQUASH AS THE FAMOUS AND OSTENSIBLY INNOCUOUS *POMADA*, LIFE AND SOUL OF MENORCAN FESTES.

razed to the ground during ferocious Turkish reprisals. Recently, the **Portal de la Llum** has been restored and several gargoyles replaced. The **Palau Episcopal** adjoins the rear of the cathedral.

Before proceeding on to Es Born, or main square, it is well worth making a detour through the labyrinth of back streets that are steeped in the medieval history of the city. Facing the west entrance to the cathedral, the **Palau Olives** and a little further on, on Carrer St. Sebastià, the **Palau Squella**. On Carrer Sta. Clara , the **Palau Lluriach**, home of Menorca's oldest titled family, the Barons de Lluriach, and the **Convent of Sta. Clara** whose tales of martyrs, arson and abductions form an intrinsic part of Ciutadella's history.

Carrer Roser, on the other side of the **Pla de la Seu**, leads us to the **church of Our Lady of the Rosary** with its ornately decorated barroque doorway, site of the municipal art gallery. On Carrer Bisbe Vila, one of the **Saura palaces**, occupied today by a bank, and beside it the renaissance Augustinian **convent of Socors**. In summer, the traditional Music Festival and auditions for the **Capella Davídica** choir are held in the cloister. In Plaça de la Llibertat a picturesque open-air market is held daily alongside the newly-built Casa de Cultura. On Carrer Santíssim, two more interesting palaces: the **Palau de los Duques de Almenara Alta** and the **Palau Saura**, part of which has been converted into an antique shop. Carrer St. Francesc, Carrer Palau and Carrer St. Jeroni, all of which lead to Carrer Major de Born, form what was once *el Call* or Jewish quarter.

On arrival at the Pl. del Born, we come across the obelisk built in memory of the victims of the Turkish attack. The shadow it casts, like that of a sundial, points in turn to the many notable buildings that surround the square. To our left as we enter the square, the **Palaus de Salort** and **Vivó** and, further on, the **convent of St. Francesc**. To the right, the **Palau del Conde de Torre Saura**, probably the most splendid of all the mansions. Just beyond, the **Teatre des Born** and its neighbour, the **Cercle Artístic**. On the next block, to round off the ensemble, the **Town Hall**, built in the 19th century on the site of the Moorish governor's citadel. From the rear of this building there is a magnificent view over the port.

On the map we may observe that the interior of Sa Contramurada, the area we have dealt with up to now, opens onto a wide avenue which runs

View of the port with es Pla de St. Joan in the background

parallel to the bay. This avenue separates Es Born from the city's other open space, the **Plaça dels Pins**, is known as the **Camí de Sant Nicolau** and terminates at the castle of the same name. Here, in the forecourt, stands a bust of the Ciutadella-born **Farragut**, navy Admiral during the American Civil War. This is a perfect spot for watching the sun go down over the distant silhouette of Mallorca on the horizon. The aspect of this whole area may change if plans for increasing the capacity of the port are carried out.

Compared to Maó harbour, the **port of Ciutadella** almost resembles a Venetian canal, complete with bridge, and its diminutive proportions have a lot to do with its charm. It is barely a kilometre in length and has an average width of two hundred metres. Towering above, the Born bastion offers a stark

background to the waterfront below with its terraces, passers-by, fishing boats and yachts that fill the little port with colourful activity. An unusual meterological phenomena takes place in the waters of the harbour from time to time, the *rissagues*. The water level drops drastically, to the point of disappearing completely, and then returns like a flash flood with sometimes catastrophic consequences for the moored boats, and even the quayside restaurants, as was the case in 1984. Scientific studies are being carried out to enable meteorologists to forecast the phenomena and thus minimize damages. From the Born area there are two ways down to the port, Portal del Mar St. just behind the Town Hall, or the steps of the Baixada Campllonch which lead towards the **Pla de St. Joan**, scene of an important part of the famous **St. Joan festivities**.

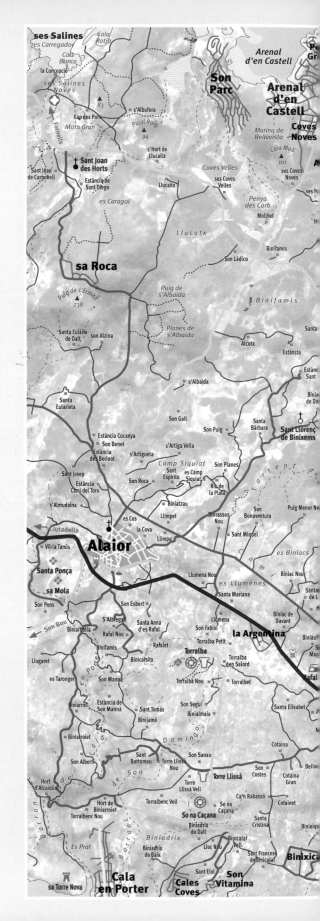

▷ **Port de Maó**
▷ **Sa Mesquida**
▷ **Es Grau**
▷ **Far de Favàritx**
▷ **Na Macaret**

The whole north-eastern coast is rugged, its con-figuration largely due to the violent action of the sea and the north wind. **Es Grau**, where the sea joins the saltwater lagoon of the **Albufera**, and **Port d'Addaia** which is formed by a natural inlet that extends more than 3 km. inland, are the only two places of shel-ter for boats along this stretch of coast. For this reason, sailors are advised to stay on the south side of the island when the wind is from the north, and even the beaches can be hazardous on rough days, despite the attrac-tions of **Sa Mesquida**, **Morella** and **Tortuga**.

The lagoon and marshlands of **S'Albufera des Grau** are an area of great interest to biolo-gists and ornithologists. Many species of wa-ter fowl come here in their thousands during the summer to make their nests and raise their young and it is an important port of call on the migratory routes. The lagoon is sepa-rated from the open sea by banks of reeds, pines and sabine trees.

Cap de Favàritx, with its lighthouse overlooking a landscape of harsh black slate, is a tremen-dous contrast to the gently rolling hills of **S'Albufera**, particularly on stormy days when it takes on an almost Dantesque appearance.

Between this coastline and the town of Alaior, the countryside is comprised of woodlands of evergreen oak and pine trees which alternate with rock formations of varied and curious forms, such as the **Penyes d'Egipte** or the **Capell de Ferro**, and is an ideal area for walk-ing on a hot day.

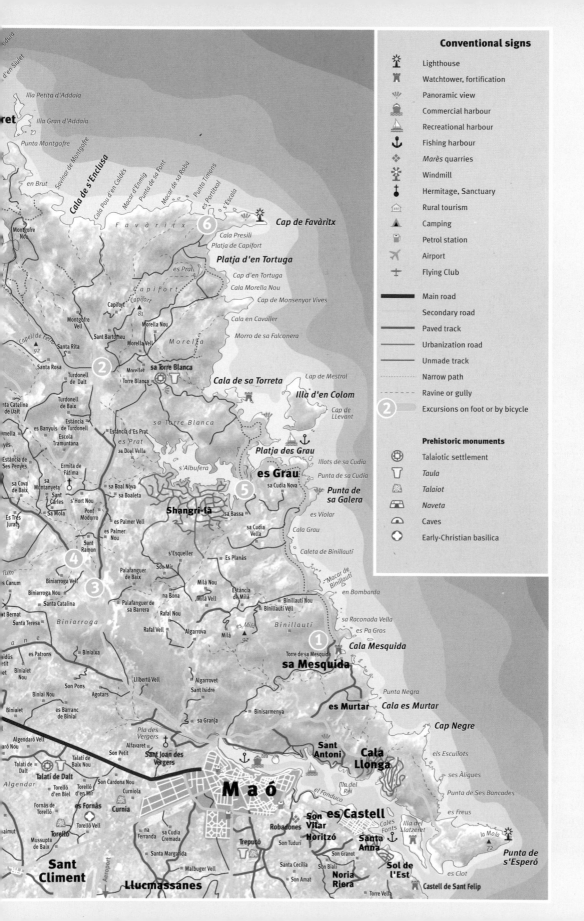

Conventional signs

- 🗼 Lighthouse
- 🏰 Watchtower, fortification
- Panoramic view
- Commercial harbour
- Recreational harbour
- ⚓ Fishing harbour
- *Marès* quarries
- Windmill
- Hermitage, Sanctuary
- Rural tourism
- ▲ Camping
- Petrol station
- ✈ Airport
- Flying Club

- ▬▬▬ Main road
- ▬▬▬ Secondary road
- ▬▬▬ Paved track
- ——— Urbanization road
- ——— Unmade track
- ········· Narrow path
- – – – Ravine or gully
- ② Excursions on foot or by bicycle

Prehistoric monuments

- Talaiotic settlement
- *Taula*
- *Talaiot*
- *Naveta*
- Caves
- Early-Christian basilica

EXCURSIONS ON FOOT
OR BY BICYCLE

1

Sa Mesquida
Es Grau

As this walk follows a clearly defined path except for occasional, short stretches, it presents no difficulty but does require some stamina and, in summer, a hat or sunshade and drinking water. There are wonderful views of the open sea and small coves that offer the welcome opportunity of a refreshing and possibly solitary swim.
To avoid having to walk all the way back, which would render this excursion impractical to all but the extremely energetic, consider the possibility of returning from **Es Grau** by bus, taxi or arrange to be met by car.
•TIME APPROX:
3-4h. (one-way)

2

Camí de Montgofre Nou

This walk takes us, there and back, from the main road to the entrance to the **Montgofre Nou** estate, which is closed to the public, and back. On the way we can see the curious rock formations of **Capell de Ferro** (Iron Hat) to the west of the path. Also possible by car.
•TIME APPROX:
Less than 1h

3

Camí de sa Boval
Torre Blanca

The Camí de sa Boval crosses an extension of farmland which once formed part of the S'Albufera marshlands. The archeological site at Torre Blanca, complete with *naveta*, remains of a settlement and *taula* (the only one with a sea view), offers lovely panoramic views of the coast and the **Illa d'en Colom**. Totally practicable by car it is one of the excursions that allows us to discover the island's interior.
•TIME APPROX:
2h 30m (return)

4

Es Puntarró
Binixems

Starting from the same flat area described in the previous excursion, we follow the path towards higher ground and a protected zone of rich woodland (recently included in the protected areas), arriving eventually at the shrine of **St. Llorenç de Binixems**, one of the island's oldest, built at the time of the Catalan conquest in the 13th century and mentioned in the Treaty of Anagni.
•TIME APPROX:
2h 30m (return)

5

Es Grau
Sa Torreta

We cross the wooden bridge that spans the narrow canal leading us to Es Grau beach. On the far side of the beach we take the path that follows the coastline. Beyond a tiny cove with a house, we continue behind the **Punta de Fra Bernat**, ignoring another path which branches to the left. As the path ascends, there are excellent views of the **Illa d'en Colom** and we will arrive eventually at the cove of **Sa Torreta** from where we will retrace our steps.
•TIME APPROX:
2h (return)

6

Favàritx
Cala Morella

After exploring the interesting scenery of the **Cap de Favàritx** headland surrounding the lighthouse, we return to **Tortuga**.
An area of dunes and marshlands (usually dry in summer) lies just behind the beach. Our objective is to reach **Morella Nou**, crossing the headland that separates the two beaches. On this walk we will come across a great variety of terrains and natural environments.
•TIME APPROX:
1h 30m (return)

Port de Maó
ES CASTELL / CALES FONTS

Maó's natural harbour stretches inland for 5 kms. giving safe anchorage to vessels of all kinds and has been highly considered by illustrious sailors over the centuries. The panoramic views from the newly built avenues high on the cornice are magnificent, and a boat trip around the port is highly recommendable and offers an alternative persepctive.

*Clustered around the bay, **Es Castell** is the first town in Spain to be awoken by the sun rise every morning. Counterpoint to this, the old fishing port of **Cales Fonts** is a busy nucleus of bars and restaurants that fill to capacity on summer nights, making this one of the island's livellest night spots.*

The **Es Pa Gros** headland, 68 mts. high, overlooks **Cala Mesquida**. The French landed here to occupy the island in 1871. At the opposite extreme of the beach, we see the Sa Mesquida defence tower, built by the British at the end of the 18th century as protection against further surprise attacks.

Sa Mesquida
Es Pa Gros / Sa Raconada Vella

*Behind **Es Pa Gros** appears another, quieter cove knows as **Sa Raconada Vella**. Fewer people come here as there is far less sand.*

To the right, the nucleus of summer holiday homes belonging to Maoneses that has existed here for centuries.

The magnificent landscape of **Es Grau** with its ample beach and traditional houses to one side and the **Illa d'en Colom** to the other, has benefitted from the declaration of the **S'Albufera** as the island's first National Park. The unique nature of this sizeable ecological zone (1790 hectares are now protected) has, at last, been recognized and scientific and educational projects, instead of buildings and developments, are planned here for the future.

Es Grau

The declaration of **S'Albufera** as a National Park emphasizes the importance of this marshland zone that forms part of the migratory routes of many European and African birds. It is connected to the sea by the narrow Sa Gola canal.

Another place of interest in this area is the quiet and secluded **Cala de sa Torreta** which can only be reached on foot from Es Grau. It marks the end of the itinerary 5 on page 42.

Es Grau

Sa Torreta / Illa d'en Colom

The **Illa d'en Colom** can be visited on the motor boat that leaves from Es Grau.

The **Caló des Moro** is one of the two small but attractive beaches to be found on the islet.

Close to Favàritx, the lovely, un-spoilt cove of **Morella Nou** is surrounded by pinewoods and a typical old boathouse stands on the beach. It can be reached following the itinerary 6 on page 42.

Cala en Tortuga (Capifort) and **Cala Presili** are two adjacent coves very popular with those who choose to escape from the beaches of the more built-up parts of the island. There is a small area of marshland just inland from Tortuga.

Far de Favàritx

MORELLA NOU / CALA D'EN TORTUGA

*The silhouette of the **Favàritx** lighthouse overlooks the black slate, almost lunar, landscape of the most desolate headland of the eastern coast. On stormy days, the sea breaking over the rocks is a breathtaking sight.*

The rugged outline of this part of the coast gives rise to hidden treasures such as the coves of **S'Enclusa** and **Montgofre**. In the background, the islets of Addaia and the fishing village of Na Macaret.

Another view of the solitary coves of **Montgofre**, largely protected from intrusion by their practical inaccessibility other than from the sea.

Na Macaret

At the mouth of the narrow and elongated **Port d'Addaia** and protected by the Illa de ses Mones islet, the pleasure harbour and, beyond, **Cala Molí** and the houses of **Na Macaret**.

The reefs that abound in the limpid waters around the **Gran** and **Petita Addaia** islets, render dangerous the entrance to the port which, in compensation, offers safe anchorage in its interior.

▷ Arenal d'en Castell
▷ Arenal de Son Saura
▷ Fornells
▷ Cap de Cavalleria
▷ Cala Pregonda

Es Mercadal is the geographic heart of this area, and **Fornells** its tourist centre. Its enormous bay, protected from the north wind and the sea by the Sa Mola promontory, is the ideal setting for all kinds of water sports. The nearby beaches, such as **Binimel·là**, are restful contrasts to the rest of the rugged coastline and **Pregonda**, because of its inaccessibility, remains hidden to all but the most determined visitors.

Owing to its very varied geological characteristics, it is impossible to generalize about the nature of this landscape: in **Cala Rotja**, in the bay of Fornells, there are copper-coloured formations (typical of the Triassic era also seen at the famous **Penya de s'Indi** or at **Cavalleria**) that are completely unrelated to the grey or black formations found close by. There is, however, one definitive common factor – the *tramuntana* wind that, in combination with the violent action of the waves it creates, erodes and changes the shape of all it touches.

This whole coastline has been declared a protected area under the Balearic Islands *Espais Naturals* legislation. Inland, **Santa Àgueda**, with its Moorish fortification, and **Monte Toro** are the two great vantage points of the island, and the countryside that lies between them, almost untouched by man, seems to have suffered no greater transformations than those imposed by the changing seasons.

7

Arenal de Son Saura Cala Pudent

A short attractive walk that starts at the extreme left of **Arenal de Son Saura** beach (looking seawards), and follows the rocky coastline to the tiny **Cala Pudent** and its transparent waters.
•TIME APPROX:
Less than 1 hr (return)

8

Camí d'en Kane

If we turn off the main road here, this stretch of the old **Camí d'en Kane** leads us through surprisingly luxuriant woodlands. An ideal excursion either on foot or by bike.
•TIME APPROX:
2h (return)

9

Santa Àgueda

An ancient cobblestone road leads us to the top of the mountain at 264 metres above sea level where the most notable traces of the Moorish domination of the island are to be found in the form of a ruined fort. It has been declared part of the National Historic and Artistic Heritage and restoration work is planned for the near future. Spectacular views.
•TIME APPROX:
1h 15m (return)

10

Ferreries Camí de Ruma

Heading north from Ferreries, the **Camí de Ruma** crosses the Hort de St. Patrici estate and, after a succession of uphill bends, we arrive at St. Francesc where we must leave the car and take the unmade path to the right which will afford us excellent and unusual views of both the north and south coasts on either side. Beyond St. Josep, the pathway becomes a rough track but presents no difficulty, and the rest of the circuit, which coincides partly with the **Camí de Tramuntana**, is easy to follow, becoming steeper beyond St. Antoni de Ruma. During this last stretch we can enjoy good views of **Sta. Àgueda** and **S'Enclusa**
•TIME APPROX:
3h 30m

11

Ferragut beach Binimel·là

Starting from either of these beaches, this pleasant, easy walk enables us to discover this stretch of the coastline and **Cala Mica**, a cove that lies between the two.
•TIME APPROX:
1h 30m (return)

12

Binimel·là Cala Pregonda

A short walk along the coastline from **Binimel·là** beach, this is the best way to discover the beautiful **Cala Pregonda**.
•TIME APPROX:
Less than 1h (return)

13

Cala Rotja

Twenty-two kilometres out of Maó, on the Fornells road, we come across a metal gateway on the right where we must leave the car and continue on foot, following the wide, unmade path until we reach a stone wall which must be climbed. From here we will take the left fork which leads through a pine wood to the curious geological formations of **Cala Rotja**. The characteristic, red clay flats which give the beach its name (*rotja* meaning red in Catalan) are a popular site for skin-cleansing mud baths or simply for enjoying the splendid view of the great bay of Fornells. The best way to return is by following the coastline via **Cala Blanca** and, on arrival at the abandoned saltworks and old house at La Concepción, take the path that leads back to our point of departure.
•TIME APPROX:
1H 30M

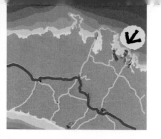

Arenal d'en Castell

Macar de sa Llosa

Arenal d'en Castell, with its many hotels and tourist developments, is protected from the east wind by the stone mass of Punta Grossa. This is one of the island's most popular beaches.

The *Macar de sa Llosa* is another lovely spot lying within the same great bay as Arenal d'en Castell, from where it may be reached on foot. Access is easier, however, from Son Parc, an urbanization situated more to the north.

Arenal de Son Saura is frequently called Son Parc, partly with reference to the tourist complex that now surrounds it, and partly in order to distinguish it from the south coast Son Saura cove. And important area of dunes lie behind the beach and , in the vicinity, the island's only golf course is to be found.

The tiny *Cala Pudent* lies to the left of Son Saura. Its proximity to the sands of the Arenal and the beauty of the surroundings make it an attractive place to visit. (See itinerary 7, page 56).

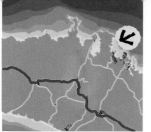

Arenal de Son Saura
Cala Pudent / La Mola de Fornells

The **Mola de Fornells** is a natural barrier between the north and northeastern coasts, and marks the northernmost point of the island. As such, the rocky headland stands as an impressive retaining wall against the violence of the sea and the fierce tramuntana.
The ample bay of Fornells and the surrounding area are protected as a nature reserve and this has prevented them from suffering the consequences of speculation and transformation.

The fishing village of **Fornells** has become an important tourist centre. The lobster calderetas served here in the restaurants have a lot to do with its popularity. The watchtower, built by the British after the demolition of the St. Antoni fort, can be seen in the background.

The installations of the old saltworks of **Ses Salines** can be seen at the end of the enormous bay of Fornells. Pinewoods almost reach the refreshing waters of **Cala Blanca** cove. *(See excursion 13 page 56).*

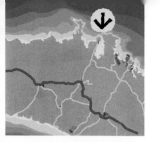

Fornells

Ses Salines / Cala Tirant

The coastline opposite the quayside is dotted with tiny coves which emphasize the impression of a land-locked sea affording ideal conditions for sailing sports of all kinds.

*At **Cala Tirant**, the name of a new urbanization, Playas de Fornells, confirms the fact that the townspeople consider this to be "their" beach. Beyond the sand, there is a marshland zone and tamarind trees.*

The **Cavalleria** peninsula ends at this headland, where the lighthouse marks the northernmost point of the island. The **Porros** islet, seen here on the horizon, is often covered by the raging sea.

The beaches of **Cavalleria** and **Ferragut** with their red sands are ideal for bathing as long as the wind is not from the north. From here to the nearby beach of Binimel·la it is a short, pleasant walk as described in the itinerary 11 on page 56.

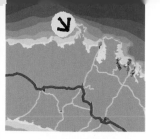

Cap de Cavalleria
FERRAGUT / SA NITJA / BINIMEL·LÀ

Another view of the **Cavalleria** headland allows us to appreciate the different configuration of the two versants: high cliffs to the east and more gentle slopes down to the sea to the west.
To the left, the old Roman port of **Sa Nitja**, where archaelogical excavations are being carried out.

Binimel·là beach is the largest and most easily accessible in an area that is well-known for the richness of its marine floor. The adjacent land, such as Es Pla Vermell, owes much of its fertility to the presence of fresh water springs.

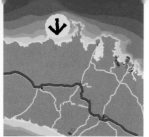

Cala Pregonda
PREGONDÓ

Inaccessibility by road has enabled **Pregonda** to remain unspoilt, conserving its idyllic combination of fine sands, transparent waters and surrounding pinewoods. The beauty of the setting is enhanced even more by its location in the centre of the rugged and inhospitable north coast. (See excursion 12 page 56).

The rocks that lie just offshore protect the cove from the open sea and would seem to have been placed there partly for this purpose and partly to add yet another attraction to this already privileged spot. The wider area of sand to the right is known as **Pregondó**.

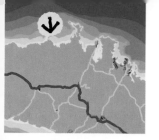

Cala Pregonda

Illes Bledes / Cala Barril
Cala Calderer

*Cala Barril is protected by another rocky crag. The larger of the **Bledes** islets undoubtedly marks the extreme of the underwater prolongation of the headland.*

*Another lovely spot on this part of the coastline, the not easily accessible **Cala Calderer** in the foreground), forms part of one of the island's largest protected areas of special interest.*

- ▷ **Cala Pilar**
- ▷ **Algaiarens**
- ▷ **Ciutadella**
- ▷ **Cap d'Artrutx**
- ▷ **Son Saura**
- ▷ **Macarella**

The western extreme of Menorca, which coincides with the municipal district of **Ciutadella**, is the driest and most barren part of the island and is bordered, to the north, by the green belt of **La Vall** and, to the south, by the gorges or ravines. It takes the shape of a great platform which slopes progressively down towards the south coast. Many prehistoric monuments are to be found in this area along with fine examples of wealthy landowners' mansions that remain today as evidence of past affluence.

The beaches on the south coast of this area have been saved from development as access to them is only possible by crossing private property. As a result, **Es Talaier**, **Turqueta** and **Macarella** are of an unspoilt, natural beauty unsurpassed almost anywhere in the Mediterranean. The beaches remain untouched thanks to the landowners' reluctance to permit entry via their estates. Access by car is controlled and limited at gates on the approach paths and, in recent times, even a charge (locally known as the "ecology tax") was made per vehicle. Here we have a classic example of a double-edged argument. If indiscriminate access to these beaches is allowed, they are in great danger of losing their unique, virgin status, but public opinion is divided and the controversy continues year after year. Apparently, the local authorities are about to take part in the issue, so, hopefully, some solution will be found in the near future.

Other beaches in the Ciutadella area such as **Cala en Blanes**, **Cala en Brut**, **Santandria**, **Cala en Forcat** and **Cales Piques**, are crowded in summer but offer all kinds of tourist attractions and services.

The city of Ciutadella with its marked Mediterranean character and aristocratic atmosphere is described in detail in its own section.

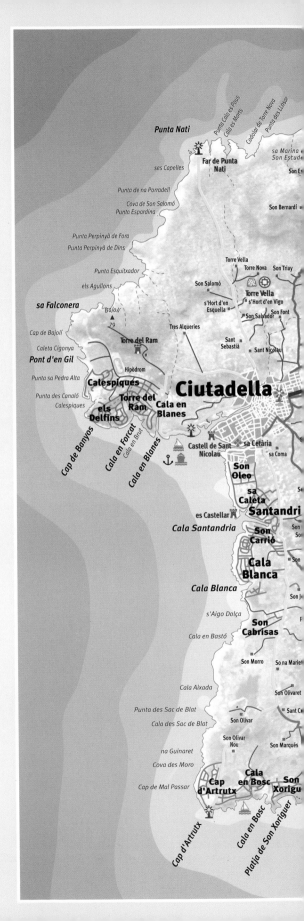

14

Els Alocs
Cala Pilar

Halfway up the cliffside, the path follows the coastline leading us to **Cala Pilar** beach, one of the most appreciated by solitary bathers who choose to escape from the crowds during the high season. There is even a freshwater spring, an added advantage at any time of year. Walking eastwards behind the Punta des Carregador, we find a curious work of nature: hundreds of rocks have been eroded by the sea to form pebbles of such disproportionate size that the beach they form has the appearance of a giant's playground.
•TIME APPROX:
2h (return)

15

Cala Galdana
Cala Macarella
Cala en Turqueta

The first stretch of the path is separated from the sea by pine woods. The beautiful coves of **Macarella** and **Macarelleta** are, in themselves, well worth the trip, but, after a refreshing swim there, it is advisable to carry on as far as **Cala en Turqueta**. If we wish to complete our discovery of the area, we can combine this walk with the one that follows, in which case we should allow another half an hour on top of the sum of the two individual timings.
•TIME APPROX:
2h 30m (return)

16

Torre Trencada
Algendar gorge

Leaving Ciutadella on the Camí Vell de Maó, we will make a first stop at **Torre Trencada** to visit the *talaiot* and *taula*. The site is well signposted and there is a car park. From here, we can walk to **Torre Llafuda** to see the smaller *taula* before returning to the car and driving to the fork that leads to the left of Son Guillem. We will leave the car where the tarmac road ends and continue, on foot, to the **Algendar gorge**. The old pathway, excavated out of the rock and still paved with cobble stones in places, leads us on an attractive walk to the gorge of the river bed, passing through luxuriant vegetation.
•TIME APPROX:
1h (return) on foot

17

Punta de s'Escullar

This short excursion brings us into contact with the northeast coast, which is rugged and solitary, except for specific points such as the nearby **Cala Morell**. Vehicles must be left where the asphalt finishes, and good views of the cliffs are to be had from the headland just beyond the road's end.
•TIME APPROX:
1h (return)

18

Son Xoriguer
Es Talaier

This walk can also be started from Cala en Bosc, crossing the built-up area that separates it from Son Xoriguer. The path is always close to the sea and several stone walls must be climbed with the aid of *botadors*, the rudimentary steps formed by protruding stones. Beyond the Son Aparets Nou estate and the entrance to Torre Saura Vell, we will encounter the ample, twin beaches of Son Saura. From here on, the track is not very clearly defined, but presents few obstacles. Passing the Punta des Governador on our right, we proceed to Es Talaier, another cove of fine, white sands, much smaller than Son Saura, but also surrounded by pine woods. The idea of combining this excursion with the previous one is worth considering.
•TIME APPROX:
3h 30m (return)

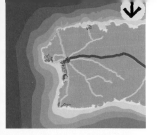

Cala Pilar
CALA CARBÓ

Although there is a good half an hour's walk to **Cala Pilar** (or perhaps for this very reason, as it discourages the majority of possible visitors) this beach is one of the most popular among those who wish to escape from the crowds. To the left of the beach, an interesting cove of giant pebbles, eroded by the sea over the centuries. (See excursion 14 page 70).

Cala Carbó is another characteristic enclave of the north coast, a small pebbled beach, hidden at the foot of the mountain. Its name – "carbó" meaning coal – comes from the charcoal stacks that were once found in the area. The ancient pathways that led to the beach have all but disappeared among the wild vegetation, and today the easiest route of access is from the sea.

The ensemble formed by the larger and smaller **Algaiarens** beaches and that of **Ses Fontanelles** is the high spot of one of the most interesting areas of the island which coincides with the **La Vall** estate. The Codolar de Biniatram appears in the background.

In **Algaiarens**, the beauty of the surrounding landscape of sand dunes and marshland combines with the clean sands and transparent waters to create an idyllic spot for bathing.

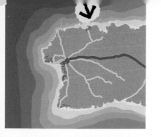

Algaiarens

CALA MORELL / PUNTA NATI

The deep inlet of **Cala Morell** offers a welcome refuge to sailors on a stretch of increasingly rugged coastline. Among the houses of the new development, a few prehistoric caves remain as proof that the cove has been inhabited by man since time immemorial.

Punta Nati is a desolate region; the lighthouse stands on a cliff that drops abruptly to the sea and nothing but the sparsest of vegetation grows among the rocks. The only buildings are "ponts", curious stone constructions that were used as shelters for livestock.

Beyond **Cap de Bajolí**, the westernmost point of the island, the natural archway of **Pont d'en Gil** appears like the secret doorway to a hidden cove.

To the north of Ciutadella, tourist developments rise like fortifications around the narrow inlet of **Cala en Forcat**.

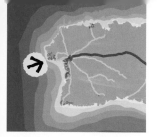

Cala en Forcat
Pont d'en Gil / Cala en Blanes

Cala en Brut is almost an estuary with hardly any sand, but sunbathers make use of the concrete platforms that litter the banks for this purpose.

Cala en Blanes is wider and deeper than the previous coves, but, even so, in summer it fills to capacity with both tourists and locals from the neighbouring Ciutadella.

The Gothic cathedral has always been the centre point of the old *Ciutadella,* but this perspective of the port will soon be a thing of the past. In the near future an ambitious project will be put into practice to enlarge the harbour far beyond its present limits in response to the ever-increasing demand for mooring space for both commercial and recreational vessels.

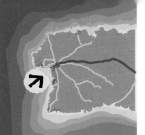

Ciutadella

Santandria is a narrow and elongated inlet which has always been Ciutadella's traditional playground. It also played an important role in the 18th C. when it became the gateway to the city under the French domination.

Cala Blanca, further to the south, is a centre for both local and visiting holidaymakers. There are prehistoric caves around both the coves.

At **Cap d'Artrutx**, the south-western extreme of the island, the land slopes gently down to the channel between Menorca and Mallorca. The Cap d'Artrutx and Capdepera lighthouses mark the coastlines of the respective islands.

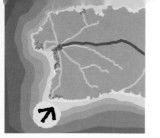

Cap d'Artrutx
Santandria / Cala Blanca
Cala en Bosc / Son Xoriguer

Cala en Bosc, the westernmost beach on the south coast, is surrounded today by holiday resorts of recent creation that include an artifical inland lake where a pleasure harbour has been built.

*The natural bay formed by **Son Xoriguer** beach is flanked, on one side by the holiday resort of the same name and, on the other, by unspoilt terrain, seen in the foreground.*

On Ciutadella's south coast, **Son Saura**, **Es Talaier**, **Turqueta** and **Macarella** comprise an area that has, fortunately, been protected from development and whose beaches remain unspoilt. Here, Son Saura, the largest of them.

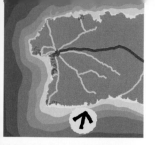

Son Saura

Es Talaier / Cala en Turqueta

Beyond Son Saura and the Punta des Governador, **Es Talaier** is a delightful spot. As in the case of the neighbouring beaches, the decomposition of the limestone soil has created the white sand that is so characteristic of this area. (See excursion 18 page 70).

On contemplating **Cala en Turqueta** and **Macarella-Macarelleta** (shown in the following double page spread) it is easy to see why these beaches are considered among the island's finest. Access to them by road is fraught with difficulties but for boats they provide safe anchorage in idyllic settings.

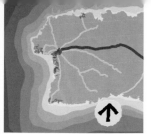

Macarella-Macarelleta

▷ Cala Galdana
▷ Trebalúger
▷ Son Bou
▷ Cala en Porter

Between the **Algendar gorge** that marks the boundary between the Ciutadella and Ferreries districts and the **Cala en Porter** gorge in Alaior, the countryside is characterized by the streams and torrents that have cleaved their way through the limestone land surface on their way to the sea.

The coastline, fairly elevated at **Cala Galdana**, drops slowly until it reaches **Binigaus**, starting point of an almost uninterrupted stretch of some of the island's most popular sandy beaches: **St. Adeodat**, **St. Tomàs**, **Atàlitx** and **Son Bou**, whose eastern extreme is marked by the cliffs at **Cap de ses Penyes**.

The limpid waters of the **Mitjana**, **Trebalúger**, **Fustam** and **Escorxada** coves are the great attraction of this area and **Cala Galdana**, despite the impact of the tourist development that has taken place there, is still the most symbolic of the Menorcan coastline. Groves of pine trees that grow down as far as the sandy beaches, emerald green waters, luxuriant vegetation and sweet-water springs combine to create an idyllic environment.

It is perhaps in this part of the island where the visitor encounters the widest and richest range of alternatives offered by nature: from long, open beaches packed with cosmopolitan tourists, easily reached from Ferreries, Es Migjorn or Alaior (see map and itineraries), to secluded coves only accessible by boat or on foot. There are hotels and appartments at **Cala Galdana**, **St. Tomàs** and **Son Bou** that offer all kinds of services and conveniences.

IV EXCURSIONS ON FOOT
OR BY BICYCLE

19

Ferreries
Algendar gorge

This is another way to visit the lovely **Algendar** gorge (see itinerary 16 on page 70). Shortly after the **Cala Galdana** junction, we must turn left and drive steeply uphill along the road which, owing to its elevation, offers good views of **S'Enclusa** to the north. Turning then in a southerly direction towards the coast, it will lead us to **Es Canaló**, where we must leave the car and continue on foot down to the river-bed. Here, we will notice a radical change in the vegetation as we penetrate the micro-climate of the *barranc,* where palm and fruit-trees, lianas and ferns grow in almost tropical profusion. Crossing the river-bed, if we have arranged for return transport, we can join the previous itinerary, in reverse direction.
•TIME APPROX:
1h (return) for the walk

20

Sant Adeodat
Cala Escorxada
Cala Fustam

The first part of this walk takes us along the beaches of **Binigaus** and then, from behind the beach bar at the mouth of the gorge, we follow the path westwards into the pine wood to **Escorxada** and **Fustam**. See Itinerary 24 as an alternative.
•TIME APPROX:
2h 30m (return)

21

Cave of Na Polida
and Cave of des
Coloms

To reach these interesting caves we must leave the car park at **St. Adeodat** and walk to **Binigaus** beach where, near the middle, a path leads us to the left towards the gorge. After about three hundred metres, we leave the main river-bed to the left, climb a wall and follow the left bank of the stream for about half a kilometre. Here, we take the fork that takes us over to the other side to the **Na Polida** cave where, with the aid of a torch, we will see extraordinary marble-like stalactites which, unfortunately, show clear signs of vandalism. From here we return to the left bank and, about half a kilometre further up, crossing back to the right, we reach the **Es Coloms** cave, also known as *Sa Catedral* owing to its size - the oval-shaped entrance is 24 metres high. Archaeological finds seem to confirm the hypothesis that this was a prehistoric sanctuary.
•TIME APPROX:
2h 30m

22

Sant Tomàs
Son Bou basilica

From one extreme to the other of these two beaches (skirting around the outside of the hotel at the end of Sant Tomàs), this is quite a long walk, although not strenuous. From **Punta d'Atàlitx** there is a good view of **Son Bou** and, at the end, we may visit the remains of the **early-Christian basilica**.
•TIME APPROX:
2h 30m (return)

23

Son Mercer de Baix,
Trebalúger and
Sa Cova gorges

The main interest of this itinerary is, not only the archaeological site at **Son Mercer de Baix**, which includes the **Cova des Moro** and other *navetes*, but also the spectacular view of the confluence of the two majestic gorges. Access by car is possible until this point, but then we must leave the car if we wish to continue down to the cave known simply as **Sa Cova** or **Son Fideu** which is most impressive.
•TIME APPROX:
1h 30m (return) for the walk.

24

Cala Galdana
Cala Trebalúger

The path leaves **Cala Galdana** and leads through pine woods to first, **Cala Mitjana** and then **Trebalúger**. If one feels up to a longer walk, it is possible to continue on as far as **St. Adeodat**. See Itinerary 20.
•TIME APPROX:
3h (return)

25

Es Migjorn
Binigaus

This alternative route to **Binigaus** beach is, in itself, a pleasant walk, particularly the last stretch that takes us along the gorge. Access is possible by car as far as the Binigaus Nou farmhouse.
•TIME APPROX:
1h 30m (return)

Cala Galdana

The surrounding landscape, rich in flora, fauna and pinewoods, and the perfect horse-shoe-shaped beach make **Cala Galdana** perhaps the most emblematic of the island's coves. In the first view, the gorges of **Algendar** and **Algendaret** can be seen as they channel their way down to the sea. In the second, the large hotel, built close to the cliff, stands as an example of the indiscriminate development of the early years of the tourist boom.

The following four photographs offer a an overall impression of the south coast beaches. Lying at the outlets of the successive gorges that cross the hinterland, they are invariably surrounded by pinewoods and the colour and transparency of the water, as seen here in **Cala Mitjana**, cannot be matched elsewhere.

The fertile soil of the **Sa Cova** barranc is exploited for vegetable and fruit farming. At the mouth of the gorge, **Trebalúger**, although a popular beach in summer, remains unspoilt thanks to its difficult access by car.

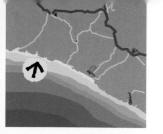

Trebalúger

CALA MITJANA / CALA FUSTAM
CALA ESCORXADA

*Another view of **Trebalúger** clearly shows how the beach acts as a separation between the sea and the approaching stream which rarely flows large enough to overcome this natural barrier. (See excursion 24 page 86).*

*Although **Fustam** and **Escorxada** are separated by the Punta de St. Antoni, the distance between them is so short that they are generally considered as a whole. The richness of the pinewoods and excellent state of conservation more than justifies their recent qualification as protected areas. (See excursion 20, page 86).*

In the central part of the south coast, the characteristic configuration of gorges and coves changes as the cliffs give way to a more gently sloping seaboard. Between the alluvial farmland and the sea, dunes are formed as seen here in **Binigaus**.

The beaches of **St. Adeodat** and **St. Tomàs** form a large resort area of hotels and appartments. This perspective, in which the opposite coastline can be seen on the horizon, serves to remind us of Menorca's size and configuration.

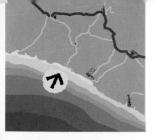

Son Bou

Binigaus / Sant Tomàs / Atàlitx

*Good panoramic views of Son Bou can be seen from the **Punta d'Atàlitx**. At this point the beach is at its narrowest but, as it is also more secluded, it is a popular spot with nudists.*

***Son Bou** is the island's longest beach (nearly 4 kms.) and also the most crowded. Its size, and the tourist attractions (including an aquatic games park) found near the hotels, make it an ideal beach for children. At the far end, an early **Christian basilica** can be visited.*

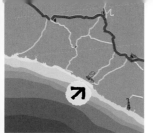

Son Bou

Beyond Cap de ses Penyes that limits Son Bou to the east, the coastline again tends towards tiny coves set among cliffs, such as **Sant Llorenç** that marks the outlet of the Torre Vella gorge.

Only the sparsest of crops grow in the shallow soil of the clifftop. Far below, the sea erodes the massive limestone block. To the left, the ruins of the **Torre Nova** watchtower built in the times of frequent pirate raids.

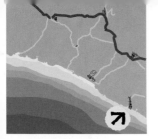

Cala en Porter
Cala Sant Llorenç / Sa Torre Nova

As it is one of the island's larger beaches, **Cala en Porter** was among the first to undergo tourist development. On the cliff face, a natural cave, **Cova d'en Xoroi**, has been converted into a discotheque and offers spectacular views of the surrounding coast.

Menorca can be unmistakably identified from the air by the geometrical shapes formed by the dry-stone walls that form one of the island's most characteristic features.

- ▷ **Cales Coves**
- ▷ **Canutells**
- ▷ **Binibèquer**
- ▷ **Punta Prima**
- ▷ **Cala Alcalfar**
- ▷ **Cala Sant Esteve**

This area is confined by, on one side, the **Cala en Porter gorge** that descends from Alaior to the sea and, on the other, by an imaginary line drawn from the innermost extreme of Maó harbour to Alaior. It is a varied landscape, although generally flat and sparsely vegetated except for the occasional area of woodland near the coast. During the winter months when rainfall tends to be high, the landscape is covered by a lush, green blanket, but the rest of the year, the twisted, dry branches of the wild olive are the most apparent element. In the gently sloping areas closer to the coast, the vegetation is more typically Mediterranean with pines and the occasional evergreen oak.

Cala en Porter, **Cales Coves**, **Es Canutells**, **Binidalí** and **Biniparratx** are examples of coves protected from the sea by high cliffs. From **Binisafúller** to **Punta Prima**, the coastline is less elevated but equally rocky. Punta Prima, the longest of these beaches, faces the **Illa de l'Aire**, the southernmost point of the island. From here to **Cala St. Esteve**, close to the mouth of Maó harbour, the coastline faces due east, and the permanent or temporary residents of **Alcalfar**, **Rafalet** and **S'Algar** are the first people in the Iberian peninsula to see the sun rise each morning.

Most of this coastline, with its many tourist developments and unspoilt hamlets, belongs to the district of **Sant Lluís**. Attempts are being made by the municipal authorities to rehabilitate the old *Camí de Cavalls*, or bridle path. Dating from 1682, it once circumvallated the whole island and one of its stretches leads from **Punta Prima** to **Alcalfar**.

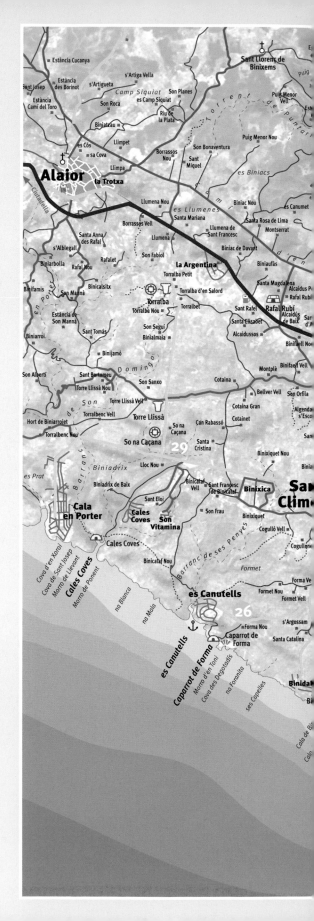

26

Forma Nou
Caparrot de Forma

Once on the **Cala Canutells** road, we must take the left fork by the **Forma Nou** farmhouse. From here, a short walk will lead us along the cliff to the Morro d'en Toni headland, from where we will see the neighbouring troglodyte caves and an ample view of the south coast.
•TIME APPROX:
30m (return)

27

Punta Prima
Rafalet gorge

Follow the coastline from the extreme left of the beach, as we look seawards, as far as the old watchtower and **Caló Roig**. Enjoying lovely views of l'**Illa de l'Aire** along the way. From here we will see the protective rocky headland of Es Torn and the houses of **Alcalfar** clustered around the bay. To the right of the main St. Lluís road we reencounter the pathway that will take us across the **S'Algar** urbanization access road. We follow this unmade track, beyond the last houses, to the gorge, and descend through the welcome shade of the dense woodland between abrupt cliff faces to the diminutive cove for a refreshing swim.
•TIME APPROX:
3h (return)

28

Sant Climent
Camí de Cotaina
Torre Llisà

This excursion brings us into contact with the characteristic landscape of rural Menorca in an area where few transformations have taken place over the years.
At Algendar we must take the turn to the left and follow the gently sloping hill past the Son Orfila and Momple farmhouses to **Cotaina**. When we reach the Alaior-Cala en Porter road, we drive across and continue to the **Torre Llisà** farm where a signpost indicates an unusual *taula*. Here we should leave the car and enter on foot so as not to disturb the farm work in progress.

29

Cales Coves

Turn off the St.Climent-Cala en Porter road at the **Son Vitamina** urbanization, leave the car when the road becomes unmade and walk down towards the sea.
The cliffs that overlook the peaceful waters of the double cove are dotted with troglodyte burial caves, many of which are inhabited in summer and some all year round. The whole necropolis has been declared a National Historic and Artistic Monument and steps are being taken to prevent its degeneration.
•TIME APPROX:
1h (return)

30

Sant Lluís
Llucmassanes
and hamlets

We leave St. Lluís on the **Punta Prima** road and take the first turning to the right which will lead us to **Torret**. The narrow road meanders through this carefully conserved hamlet and emerges on the main **Binibèquer-Binissafúller** road where we turn left through **S'Ullastrar** towards the recently excavated *taula* at **Binisafuet**. Here we turn right and continue beyond Sa Parereta where we take another right turn to follow the old Volta d'es Milord (His Lordship's Walk), as far as the **Biniparrell** junction where we turn left towards **Llucmassanes**. As high dry-stone walls flank both sides of the road during much of this circuit, better visibility will be enjoyed by bicycle than by car. If we do not wish to return via St. Lluís, there are two accesses to the main Maó-airport road.

Cales Coves

The name of *Cales Coves* is derived from the many caves excavated in the cliff walls in prehistoric times. It is believed that they were burial places but, in recent times, they have been used as living accommodation. There is a project to convert the cove into an area which may be visiited us a site of special archeological interest. The shelter afforded by this double cove means that it is usually replete with pleasure craft. (See excursion 29, page 98)

People from St. Climent and Maó were, at one time, the only visitors to **Canutells** whose small and protected beach has undergone great change in recent years.

The landscape in **Caparrot de Forma**, once uninhabited and bare, has also changed of late. The high cliffs offer splendid panoramic views of the coast. (See excursion 26, page 98)

From the sea, many caves are visible on the cliff faces where wild birds make their nests.

Canutells

Caparrot de Forma / Binidalí

*The headland to the west of **Binidalí** is another excellent viewpoint over this stretch of the coastline. Although the entrance to the cove is quite ample, the beach is diminutive but many natural platforms exist in the surrounding rocks for sunbathing or diving.*

At **Biniparratx**, the inlet describes a marked angle between the high cliff walls making it an ideal refuge for boats in bad weather. Here, too, prehistoric caves can be seen at its innermost extreme.

Beyond **Cap d'en Font**, the coastline of the St.Lluís area appears as an unbroken chain of developments and resorts. Just a few years ago, the cove at **Binissafúller** (in the foreground) comprised of no more than a few traditional weekend houses but is now surrounded by modern villas.

Binibèquer

Biniparratx / Cap d'en Font
Binisafúller / Cala Torret

The "fishing village" at **Binibeca Vell** is one of the most visited tourist attractions. Its curious construction aims to reproduce the style and use of raw materials typical of traditional Mediterranean architecture.

Binibèquer, just beyond the aforementioned village, is a beach of fine sand protected from the wind by the Morro d'en Xua headland. The following inlet is **Cala Torret**, surrounded by the resort of the same name.

Binibèquer

Biniancolla is the last of the south-facing coves. The oldest of the houses stand, literally, in the water and their ground floors are used as boathouses.

Punta Prima was appropriately named Sandy Bay by the British during their domination of the island. Always a popular holiday spot among Menorcans, the resort has grown following the building of a large hotel.

Punta Prima
BINIANCOLLA / ILLA DE L'AIRE
ALCALFAR

The **Illa de l'Aire** which rises no more than 15 m. above sea-level at its highest point near the light-house, is home to a subspecies of endemic black lizards.

The little cove at **Alcalfar**, another favourite among Menorcans, was the site of the island's first tourist-orientated hotel. The defense tower stands as proof of its strategic importance in times gone by.

S'Algar is a well-established resort situated on a rocky headland eroded by the sea. The absence of a beach is more than made up for by the many facilities available to the visitor. The tiny Cala Rafalet lies just beyond.

Although the cove of **Cala Rafalet** affords barely enough space to spread out a couple of beach towels, the beauty of the grove of holm oaks through which one passes on the way to the sea, and the views over the cliffs, more than warrant the walk.

Cala Rafalet

S'ALGAR / CALA SANT ESTEVE
LA MOLA DE MAÓ

Cala **St. Esteve** is surrounded by the military fortifications that speak to us of Menorca's turbulent history. The recently renovated Fort Marlborough (to the right) can be visited as can the military museum that stands in what remains of the legendary Castell de St. Felip.

Returning to our starting point, the old fortress of **La Mola de Maó** overshadows the southernmost headland of the south coast. Its location has lost the strategic importance of times gone by, and, today, its monumental proportions, seen here in the view of the Punta de s'Esperó, appear to peaceably-stand guard over Menorca and all her treasures.

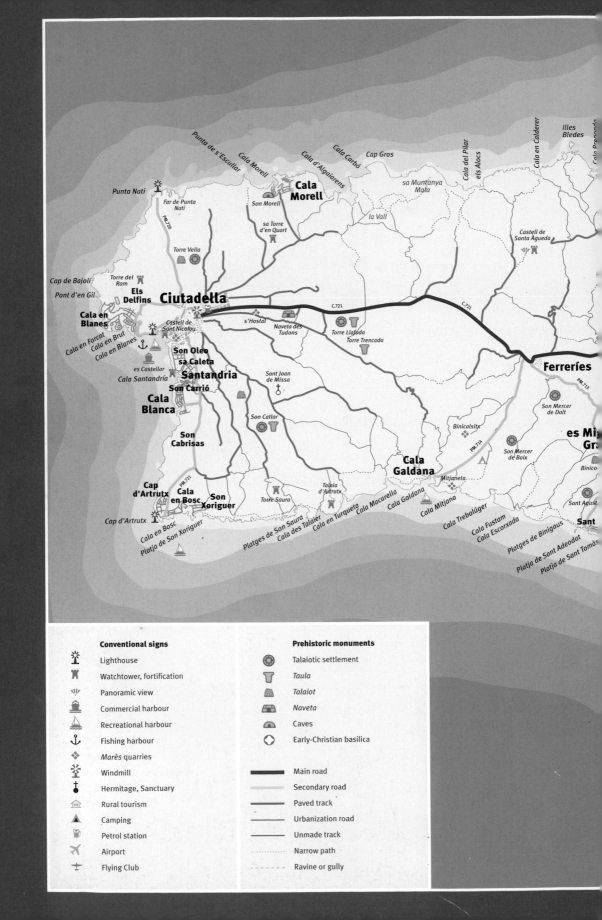

Conventional signs

- ☀ Lighthouse
- ♜ Watchtower, fortification
- �★ Panoramic view
- ⚓ Commercial harbour
- ⛵ Recreational harbour
- ⚓ Fishing harbour
- ❖ *Marès* quarries
- ☀ Windmill
- ☦ Hermitage, Sanctuary
- 🏛 Rural tourism
- ▲ Camping
- ⛽ Petrol station
- ✈ Airport
- ✈ Flying Club

Prehistoric monuments

- ◉ Talaiotic settlement
- ⊤ *Taula*
- ▲ *Talaiot*
- ⌂ *Naveta*
- ⌒ Caves
- ◇ Early-Christian basilica

- ▬▬▬ Main road
- ▬▬▬ Secondary road
- ▬▬▬ Paved track
- ───── Urbanization road
- ───── Unmade track
- ·········· Narrow path
- ‒ ‒ ‒ ‒ Ravine or gully

Menorca

orros

Cap de Cavalleria
Far de Cavalleria

nta des
au

sa Nitja

Talaia
Mola de Fornells

Fornells

Cala Tirant

Platges de Fornells
ses Salines

Arenal de S'Olla

Son Parc

Punta Grossa
Arenal d'en Castell

na Macaret

Coves Noves

Addaia

Port d'Addaia

Cap de Favàritx

Platja d'en Tortuga

C.723

PM.710

PM.710

Sant Joan des Horts

es Mercadal

sa Roca

Mare de Déu del Toro

PM.707

PM.711

C.721

PM.710

sa Torreta

Sant Llorenç de Binixems

Illa d'en Colom

PM.715

PM.712

Ermita de Fàtima

s'Albufera

Platja des Grau

es Grau

Shangri-là

Alaior

Santa Ponça

710-2

e Solí

La Argentina

Rafal Rubí

Cala Mesquida

ume rani

Torralba d'en Salord

sa Mesquida

Bou

Basílica de Son Bou

Torre d'en Gaumès

C.721

Sant Joan des Vergers

710-1

Cala Llonga

So na Caçana

Torre Llissà

Talatí de Dalt

es Fornàs

Curnía

Maó

Port de Maó

Cala en Porter

PM.704

Binixica

Torelló

PM.703

es Castell

la Mola
Punta de s'Esperó

sa Torre Nova

Cales Coves

Son Vitamina

Sant Climent

Llucmassanes

Trepucó

Castell de Sant Felip
Cala Sant Esteve
Fort Malborough

Cala en Porter

Cova d'en Xoroi

Cales Coves

Cales Coves

Aeroport

PM.702

es Cànutells

Sant Lluís

Trebalúger

Torre d'en Penjat

Caparrot de Forma

Binissafullet

s'Ullastrar

Caló des Rafalet

Cala des Cànutells

Binidalí

Cap d'en Font

Torret

PM.702

s'Algar

Alcalfar

Cala de Binidalí
Cala de Biniparratx

Binibèquer Vell

Torret de Baix

Cala d'Alcalfar

Cala de Binissafúller

Biniancolla

Punta Prima

Son Ganxo

Platja de Punta Prima

Cala de Binibèquer

Cala de Biniancolla

Illa de l'Aire

Car tours

Sa Torreta taula, from the air

1 FROM MAÓ TO SON PARC

- LA MOLA ▸ CALA MESQUIDA
- ES GRAU ▸ FAVÀRITX
- ADDAIA ▸ NA MACARET
- ARENAL D'EN CASTELL ▸ SON PARC

Starting from the innermost extreme of the port, **Sa Colàrsega**, the PM-710-1 road leads behind the power station and naval base, above the villas in Cala Rata and Cala St. Antoni and close by the colonial-style **Golden Farm** (allegedly a temporary residence of Lord Nelson, which can best be appreciated from the other side of the harbour). From here, or from the neighbouring **Cala Llonga** urbanization, we can enjoy splendid views of the city of Maó and Es Castell.

Further on, we arrive at **La Mola**, the fortress built during the reign of Isabel II to take the place of the demolished Castell de St. Felip which had stood on the opposite shore. Permission to visit La Mola, a restricted military zone, may be obtained from the Military Government in Maó.

From this point, the **Els Freus** isthmus, we can see the walled precint of **El Llatzeret**, which became an island in 1900 as a result of the opening of the Alfons XII, or St. Jordi, Canal. We will have a better view of the Llatzeret when we retrace our steps towards the Cala Mesquida junction where we will turn right. It is on the low hills of this regions where Menorca's finest camomile can be picked.

Cala Mesquida is a nucleus of traditional holiday houses and jetties clustered around the little **Sa Raconada** bay with **Sa Mesquida** beach just beyond and an 18th century watchtower overlooking from above. From here, we return to Maó and start the second phase of our tour by taking the PM-710-2 road towards Es Grau.

This road diverts from the PM-710 Fornells road just beyond the **Pla des Vergers**, or Pla de Sant Joan, vegetable gardens, which we pass on our left, and travels northwards through uneven terrain right up to the beach and village of **Es Grau** from where we may choose to take a boat trip over to **Illa d'en Colom**. **S'Albufera**, a sea-water lagoon of notable interest to biologists and naturalists, is another point of notable interest. (See excursion 5 on page 42) To continue our tour, we must return to the junction with the PM-710 road and follow it 8 kms. to the **Hermitage of Fàtima**.

About 500 metres beyond, we turn right on the PM-715 road, as if following the direction indicated by a curiously shaped craggy rock known as **Sa Sella**, the Saddle, that stands alone in the middle of the plain. At the end of this road we come to **Cap de Favàritx** and the lighthouse of the same name. The last stretch is in rather poor condition, but the unusual, almost lunar landscape of black slate, eroded by the sea for millennia, more than makes up for the uncomfortable drive. The superb beaches of **Presili** and **Tortuga** lie just to the south of the headland and can be reached by a another rough, unmade road.

We return again to the PM-710 road and after about five km. take the turning to the right which leads us, first to **Port d'Addaia**, a long, narrow bay that penetrates more than three km. inland through a richly wooded area, **Na Macaret** where many people from Alaior have their holiday homes and boathouses and, finally, the beach and modern urbanization of **Arenal d'en Castell** with its hotels and tourist developments.

Son Parc is the next place to be visited. An important tourist centre, here Menorca's only golf course is to be found along with various complexes of appartments and villas which surround the magnificent beach of **Son Saura**, or Arenal de s'Olla. To round off our tour, we will return to Maó by an alternative route, turning right at the Na Macaret-Addaia junction along the **Camí Vell d'Alaior** which leads us to the **Camí d'en Kane**. This drive offers the chance to appreciate the marked differences between the coast and the rural inland scenery of luxuriant woods of pines and evergreen oaks, farmsteads and old mansions.

2 FROM ALAIOR TO CAP DE CAVALLERIA

► MONTE TORO ► BINIMEL·LÀ
► PREGONDA ► CAVALLERIA
► CALA TIRANT ► FORNELLS ► SA ROCA

Our starting point is the higher part of the town of Alaior where the recently paved **Camí d'en Kane** passes by the cemetery and then leads towards **Es Mercadal**. We pass through some woody areas and cross the **Pla d'Alaior** with its curious rock formations that stand out in the flat landscape, basically dedicated to cattle farming, with **Monte Toro** soon appearing ahead of us.

On arrival at Es Mercadal we will take another recently repaired road which winds its way up to the top of **Monte Toro**, Menorca's highest geographical point. From here we can enjoy a complete view of the surrounding island and visit the hermitage dedicated to Our Lady. (See page 8)

We return to Es Mercadal and, ignoring the signposts to Fornells, look for the sign that reads **Platges Costa Nord** (north coast beaches) which will lead us to the **Camí de Tramuntana**. This road takes us

through an important agricultural area and, following the contours of the hills, offers wider, more panoramic views than is usual on the island. Generally, visibility from the roads is limited by the ever-present dry-stone walls. This is an interesting drive at any time of year, each season bringing with it a new colour scheme.

Follow the **Binimel·là** and **Pregonda** signposts which indicate roads or tracks to the right. The drive to Binimel·là is worthwhile in itself and the beach, in summer, is the perfect place for a refreshing swim or a drink at the beach bar. Worthily considered to be the jewel of the north coast, Pregonda can only be reached on foot. See excursion 12 of page 56 for more details.

Our next destination is **Cap de Cavalleria**, perhaps the island's most impressive scenario where the effect of the notorious *tramuntana*, or north wind, is most manifest. The lighthouse stands on a rocky headland where goats subsist on the few sparse shrubs that manage to survive in such inhospitable terrain. It is a sheer ninety metre drop to the sea below. From the cliff-top the views of the coast are most spectacular, particularly when the *tramuntana* and the sea combine to demonstrate the forces of nature at full blast. Care should be taken if venturing near the cliff edge on windy days.

On the way back from the lighthouse, on the right-hand side of the road, lies the little port of **Sa Nitja**, site of first, Phoenician, and then Roman settlements. The remains of an early Christian basilica are to be found near the watchtower on the Es Brau headland opposite. We will now head towards Fornells, maybe stopping on the way to visit the rapidly developing tourist centre of **Cala Tirant** and the marshland zone which lies just inland.

Fornells is the safest port to be found on the rugged north coast and, as such, is invariably packed with boats, and the ample bay is ideal for windsurfing. Owing to the rapid growth of tourism, Fornells has been transformed from a sleepy fishing village to a busy, cosmopolitan town. Nevertheless, it retains much of its picturesque charm and offers pleasant strolls through the old streets or out along the quay where a watchtower dating from the British occupation still stands. No visit to Fornells is complete without trying the famous *caldereta de llagosta* at one of the many waterfront restaurants.

Leaving Fornells on the C-723 towards Es Mercadal. we then turn off on the PM-710 towards Maó until we reach the junction with the access road to the **Sa Roca** urbanization. This road will lead us back to Alaior, passing through woodlands and the **Hermitage of Sta. Ester** on the way.

Fornells

3 AROUND CIUTADELLA

- ▶ PUNTA NATI ▶ CALA MORELL
- ▶ ALGAIARENS ▶ CAP D'ARTRUTX
- ▶ CALA EN BOSC ▶ SON XORIGUER
- ▶ CALA EN TURQUETA
- ▶ CALA MACARELLA

From Ciutadella it is impossible to visit the three neighbouring coastal areas without repeatedly returning to the city as no circular road exists. Several separate excursions are therefore necessary.

The first starts at the Sa Font bastion from where we take the PM-720 to **Punta Nati**. The road is not in very good condition, but the trip is worth making as it takes us through some interesting countryside. After a few cultivated plots of land, the landscape becomes quite desolate and beyond the **Torre Vella** estate, where various *talaiots* are found, there is nothing but stone as far as the eye can see. The lighthouse, with a few surrounding bunkers, overlooks the rugged coastline, infamous for the many shipwrecks that have taken place here through the centuries. Here, Egyptian vultures, a bird of prey now extinct on the rest of the islands, can still be seen flying overhead and another curiosity of the area are *ponts*, strange stone constructions built as shelters for livestock. Just before the lighthouse there is a particularly notable, seven-tiered *pont* with a perfectly formed vault inside. Engraved in the stone, the builder's name and the date, 1857.

For our second tour, we leave Ciutadella's industrial estate on the road to **Cala Morell** and **Algaiarens**, the old **Camí de La Vall**. Along the first stretch of the road, what were once modest constructions for storing farming implements have been converted into chalets with vegetable gardens and orchards. Ahead, the fortified tower of **Torre d'en Quart**, after which we must take the road to the **Cala Morell** urbanization. From here, on the rock face of the gorge, we can

see the caves of the prehistoric necropolis, some of which have elaborate entrances. The cove beneath is protected by impressive cliffs. Returning to the junction, we continue the way we were travelling to approach **La Vall d'Algaiarens**. This is a huge estate whose owners traditionally allowed families from Ciutadella to camp here in the woods close to the beautiful beach. Entry is now restricted by a timetable that finishes at 7 p.m., but it is still possible to park here and enjoy the lovely surroundings. The luxuriant pinewoods and the marshlands have recently been catalogued as of special interest to the environment.

For the third excursion we will leave Ciutadella from the Plaça dels Pins and head south along the PM-721. The scenery here, being a more built-up area, is very different from what we have previously seen of the environs of Ciutadella. Beyond the **Cala Santandria** urbanization we can stop at **Cala Blanca**, the best beach in the area, and then continue on to our destination at **Cap d'Artrutx**. To reach the lighthouse it is worthwhile turning off the main road to the right onto the road that borders the urbanization along the coastline which here, in contrast to what we have seen at Punta Nati, is low-lying and hardly rises above sea-level. On clear days, particularly at sunset, we will see the outline of

Sant Joan de Missa

Mallorca in the distance. Continuing beyond the lighthouse, we cross the urbanizations of **Cala en Bosc** and **Son Xoriguer** to the beach of the same name whose fine, white sands are characteristic of the south coast.

The last of the Ciutadella-based excursions must be, in turn, subdivided into three, and they all start from the **Camí Vell de St. Joan** near the Canal Celat.

(1) For the first, we branch off at Son Vivó towards the Son Saura beach to visit the archaeological site at **Son Catlar** with its *taula*, *talaiots* and walled precint. Access to **Son Saura** beach is complicated as the road is barred by numerous gates which must be opened and closed behind us, making this trip worth-

Pont, near Punta Nati

while only if we intend to spend several hours or the entire day there.

(2) Retracing our steps to Son Vivó, we turn to the right towards the **St. Joan de Missa Hermitage** and take the Camí to Son Camaró in the direction of **Cala Turqueta**. Despite the fact that the road is unmade beyond the entrance to the Sa Marjal Nova estate, the beach is easily accessible, has a car park and is one of the island's loveliest.

(3) We must return again to the hermitage with its crenallated façade and then head towards **Macarella-Macarelleta**. Along this road, which is unmade beyond the Torralba farmhouse, we will come across very few buildings as it passes through an area of large farming estates and pastures. The coves of Macarella and Macarelleta, both closely surrounded by dense pinewoods, are two more prime examples of the island's natural beauty. As such they have become increasingly popular with both islanders and visitors alike and, in summer, have bar facilities. During the rest of the year they are almost deserted and truly idyllic.

Before closing this section, we would make one final recommendation. While travelling on the C-721 from Ciutadella to Maó, follow the signs to the **Naveta des Tudons** and the **Torre Llafuda** settlement which are further described in the Archaeology chapter.

4 FROM ES MERCADAL TO CALA GALDANA

▸ ES MERCADAL ▸ ES MIGJORN
▸ SANT TOMÀS ▸ SANT ADEODAT
▸ FERRERIES ▸ CALA GALDANA

The C-723 road that leaves Es Mercadal by the barracks leads us through a valley surrounded by high hills and tall pine trees and arrives at **Es Migjorn** alongside the beginning of the **Binigaus gorge** whose fertile slopes have been terraced for farming. This drive offers a different landscape from most of the island, being almost reminiscent of a mountainous area. Along the way we pass several old houses built on top of hillocks, probably for defensive purposes. The town of Es Migjorn is well worth a visit before continuing on to the beaches of **St. Tomàs**, **St. Adeodat** and their tourist developments. On the way, we will pass, on our left the prehistoric settlements of **Sta. Mònica** and, on our right, **St. Agustí** with a curious, hollow *talaiot* whose roof is supported by a central pillar.

On returning to Es Migjorn, and before continuing on towards Ferreries, we can visit the *talaiots* at **Binicodrell de Darrera** by taking the old Camí de Binigaus, near the cemetery. Back on the main road, it is a pleasant drive to Ferreries and a good view of the whole town can be seen just beyond the turning that leads to **Son Mercer** (see excursion 23 on page 86)

From Ferreries we take the C-721 in the Cala Galdana direction and then, just outside the town, turn left on the PM-714 which will lead us between the **Algendar** and **Trebalúger gorges**. We will pass on our left, first the turning which leads to **Cala Trebalúger** and then another which leads to **Cala Mitjana**. From the outskirts of Cala Galdana, the road drops quite steeply down to the beach which is surrounded by woodland and protected from the open sea by high cliffs. The mouth of the **Algendar gorge** serves as a canal for the mooring of small boats. Despite the presence of hotels and appartments complexes that have brought mass tourism to **Cala Galdana**, the natural beauty of the surroundings still place it among the most attractive of the south-coast beaches.

Sant Adeodat

5 SOUTH-EASTERN AREA

▸ Talatí ▸ Rafal rubí ▸ Son bou
▸ Torre d'en Gaumés
▸ Torralba d'en Salord
▸ So na Caçana ▸ Cala en Porter
▸ Sant climent ▸ Canutells
▸ Binibèquer ▸ Sant lluís
▸ Punta prima ▸ Alcalfar ▸ Sant esteve

On this tour we will have the opportunity to visit several archaeological sites. We take the C-721 Maó to Alaior road and turn left just beyond the airport junction to **Talatí de Dalt** with its notable *taula* with lateral leaning pillar, a large, circular *talaiot*, and several burial caves. On our way back to the main road, on a turning to the right, we can see the two *navetes* of **Rafal Rubí**.

At the junction just outside Alaior, we turn left on the road to **Son Bou**, the island's longest beach. The demand for tourist accommodation has resulted in the drastic reduction of the marshland area, **Es Prat de Son Bou**, situated behind the beach, part of which once served as rice-fields. From **St. Jaume**, the overlooking hill, now a densely built-up area, there is a splendid view of such panoramic proportions that one can, almost, ignore the two monstruous, high-rise hotels that invade the horizon to our left. Apart from the usual tourist attractions, there is an aquatic games park near the hotels, an interesting early Christian basilica (see pages 20 and 86) and some excavated caves.

On our way back towards Alaior, we will make a detour to the right to **Torre d'en Gaumés**, one of the most complete of the prehistoric settlements. Apart from the large *talaiots*, there is much more to see, such as the enormous hypostyle chamber and the channels and water tanks that formed part of a drainage system. When this site was excavated, a 15 cm. bronze statue (circa 600 BC) of the Egyptian deity **Imhotep** was found, along with other elements dating from prehistory through both the Roman and Moor-ish occupations. From here it is a short walk to the megalithic tomb at **Ses Roques Llisses**.

From Alaior we will take the **Cala en Porter** road, stopping twice on the way at archaeological sites. At the first, **Torralba d'en Salord**, conservation work has recently been carried out by the *Fundació Illes Balears* whose well-documented, explicative pamphlets are available at the site. Passing **Torre Llisà Vell** on our right (see excursion 28 on page 98), just before the junction with the St. Climent road, we come to **So na Caçana** where we will see a *talaiot* crowned, curiously, by a geodetic measuring instrument. Findings here suggest that this was an important religious centre but, today, for some reason it is one of the less-visited sites.

Cala en Porter suffered the consequences of anarchic and excessive growth during the first years of the tourist boom and, although, an effort has been made to rectify some of the worst mistakes, it remains today as an example of man's insensitivity to his surroundings. Half-way up the cliff to the left of the beach, the **Cova d'en Xoroi** is well worth a visit, particularly in the early evening to watch the sunset from the balconies, or at night for the romantic moonrises. During the summer it is transformed in the evening into a discotheque. The cave is home to one of Menorca's most popular folk legends: that of Xoroi, an earless Moor who lived here with a girl he abducted from one of the farms and their three children. The footprints left by him in the snow while out foraging for food, led soldiers to the hideaway, whereupon,

Detail of rural architecture

to avoid capture and enslavery, Xoroi and the eldest son leapt to their deaths in the sea below.

From **Cala en Porter**, we will continue via **St. Climent** to Cala **Canutells** situated at the mouth of a gorge and important tourist centre. The entire coastline of the **St. Lluís** area, to be visited next, is an almost continuous succession of urbanizations from **Binidalí** to **Punta Prima**. Set further back from the sea, and usually on rises in the ground, we will see a number of large old mansions overlooking the coast.

At **Cala Binidalí** there is an excellent viewpoint at the top of the cliff that overlooks the cove. Along with the neighbouring **Biniparratx**, it is one of the deepest in proportion to its width, and burial caves are seen in the rocks behind both beaches. In summer they are packed to capacity by boats taking advantage of the shelter afforded by these singular havens.

From here on, the coastline is less rugged and flatter beyond **Cap d'en Font**. Between the beaches of **Binisafúller** and **Binibèquer**, we come across the curious resort of **Binibeca Vell**, built to imitate the traditional architectural forms of the old fishing villages. The last beach in this area, **Punta Prima** in the extreme south-east corner of the island was popular among the islanders before the appearance of tourism and known at the time of the British occupation as Sandy Bay. Opposite, the **Illa de l'Aire**, famous for its lighthouse and indigenous black lizards, offers spectacular views in all weathers. There are bars and restaurants in the vicinity of all the aforementioned beaches. By turning right off the Punta Prima-St. Lluís road, we will arrive at **Cala Alcalfar** and **S'Algar**. The former was the island's pioneer tourist resort, whereas S'Algar, with its hotels, villas and appartments is of more recent development and offers many services such as tennis, horse-riding, deep-sea diving and parascending.

Before returning to Maó, our last stop will be **Cala St. Esteve**, where the restored Malborough fort may be visited, and **Es Castell**, perhaps rounding off the day with dinner at one of the popular waterfront restaurants in **Cales Fonts**.

Cala Alcalfar

The little harbour at Binibeca Vell

Information
and suggestions

THE AIM OF THIS SECTION IS NOT TO SUPPLY A LIST OF PRACTICAL DATA AND ADDRESSES WHICH GENERALLY TEND TO BE CHANGEABLE AND, AS A RESULT, OFTEN MISLEADING. RELIABLE, UP TO DATE INFORMATION OF THIS NATURE CAN BE OBTAINED FROM LOCAL OFFICIAL SOURCES. WE WOULD, HOWEVER, LIKE TO MENTION A FEW THINGS THAT MAY HELP TO MAKE YOUR VISIT TO THE ISLAND MORE ENJOYABLE, AND YOUR DISCOVERY OF ITS CHARACTER AND CUSTOMS MORE COMPLETE AND REWARDING.

ART AND CULTURE

THE ATTRACTION THE ISLAND HAS ALWAYS HELD FOR ARTISTS IS MADE MANIFEST BY THE NUMBER OF THEM, BOTH OF LOCAL STOCK AND OUTSIDERS, WHO HAVE SOUGHT AND FOUND INSPIRATION IN THESE UNIQUE SURROUNDINGS OVER THE CENTURIES.

PAINTING

Painting has always been a particularly fruitful field with a marked emphasis on landscape painting in which the island's special quality of light has always played an important role. In the 18th century, the Italian **Giuseppe Chiesa** (1720-1789), who set up residence here following his marriage to a Menorcan woman, left an important pictorial record of the island at that time and introduced the Italian naturalist influence known as *veduta*. His Menorcan disciple

Pascual Calbó (1752-1817) was famous for both his scientific treatise and his artistic qualities. In the nineteenth century, the wide seascapes of Maó harbour under stormy skies, painted by **Font** (1811-1885), were recurrent examples of the romantic school of the time. **Hernández Monjo** (1862-1937) also left a legacy of seascapes, full of light and colour, in this case in the turn of the century modernist style.
Contemporary art is represented by two important landscape painters: **Joan Vives Llull** (1901-1982) in whose impressionist work nature is the most important element, and **Josep Torrent** (1904-1990), Ciutadella-born expressionist, whose original technique captures the essence and rhythm of the island. Also from Ciutadella, **Maties Quetglas** (1946), who has lived and worked in Madrid for some years, is known both nationally and internationally among the hyperrealist school.
Works by these, and other artists of more recent apparition, may be viewed at the following:

ART GALLERIES AND MUSEUMS

MAÓ:

Museu de Menorca. The old Convent of St. Francesc, Av. Dr. Guàrdia. Worth visiting for the building itself and its contents. Important exhibitions of the island's archaeological heritage, fine arts, ethnology and a library. Tel. 971 35 09 55.
Museu Hernández Sanz – Hernández Mora. In the Claustre del Carme. Maps and engravings dating from the seventeenth to nineteenth centuries, paintings and an important library. Tel. 971 35 05 97.
Sala de Cultura "Sa Nostra", situated in the old St. Antoni church, S'Arraval 32, holds temporary exhibitions all year round.

The **Scientific, Literary and Artistic Athenaeum.** Rovellada de Dalt 25. Works by *Vives Llull,* collections of drawings and paintings, Menorcan natural history exhibition. Cultural and sociological lectures are given all year round. Tel. 971 36 05 53.
Galeria Artara. Rosario 18.
Fortalesa de la Mola. Guided tours, information Tel. 971 36 21 00.

CIUTADELLA:

Sala Municipal in the Roser church on the street of the same name. Exhibitions.
Sala de Cultura "Sa Nostra" in the St. Josep church on C/Sta.Clara. Exhibitions.
Galeria Retxa. Seat of a collective group of artists with temporary exhibitions by others.
Museu Municipal Bastió de sa Font, Pla de sa Font, Tel. 971 38 02 97. Historical, archaeological and ethnological exhibits.
Museu Diocesà, adjoined to the Seminary. Pere Daura collection of contemporary painting, rare and antique exhibits of historical and religious value.
Casa-Museu Pintor Torrent, C/St Rafael.
Castell de Sant Nicolau. Tel. 971 38 10 50.
Pedreres de s´Hostal. Run by "Líthica", an association dedicated to the protection of stone quarries, this is an interesting ensemble of both the oldest and newest quarries just two km. from Ciutadella on the Camí Vell de Maó. Recommended itineraries are well signposted within the site. Tel. 971 48 15 78.

ALAIOR:

Centre de Cultura de Sant Diego. In the old St. Diego church.
Sala Municipal d'Art Contemporani, Major 11. Tel. 971 37 10 02.
Galeria Arths. Costa de l'Església 11.

ES MERCADAL:

Ecomuseu de Cap de Cavalleria. Situated in the privileged surroundings of the Santa Teresa estate, this small museum offers the chance to discover the Roman history of Menorca, brought to light by the Sanisera excavations. Tel. 971 35 99 99. **Espai Hartung**, C/Vicari Fuxà. Summer exhibitions.

ES MIGJORN GRAN:

Johanna Byfield. C/St. Llorenç 12-14.

FERRERIES:

Museu de la Natura de Menorca. C/ Mallorca, 2. Tel. 971 37 45 05 / 971 35 07 62.

SANT LLUÍS:

Es Molí de Dalt. The old windmill has been restored to full working order and contains an interesting exhibition of farming implements. Tel. 971 15 10 84.

ES CASTELL:

Pedrera d'en Robadones. "Centre del Patrimoni Marítim de Menorca". Here, in the largest of the subterranean quarries, more than forty traditional Menorcan vessels are on show. Camí d'en Verd, Tel. 639 601 354. **Museo Militar.** Plaça Esplanada. Tel. 971 36 21 00 / 971 36 59 47. **Castell de Sant Felip.** 971 36 21 00. **Museo Fort Malborough.** Cala Sant Esteve. Tel. 971 36 04 62.

MUSIC

The visitor may be surprised by the variety of musical activities that take place on the island and, indeed, by the very high standard of the performances. Menorcans are, by tradition, a music-loving people.

OPERA AND CLASSICAL MUSIC

Every year in the spring, the **Amics de l'Òpera** hold an Opera Week, the *Setmana de l'Òpera*, traditionally in the incomparable setting of the Teatre Principal. Another very active group is **Joventuts Musicals**. From October to May they give concerts on alternate Mondays in the St. Josep church in Ciutadella and in Sta. María in Maó. During July and August they hold **Summer Music Festivals** which take place, in Maó in the Cloister of St. Francesc, and in Ciutadella in the Cloister of the Seminary. The nature of both these locations enhance the quality of the performances. During the last two weeks of July, in the *Aules de Cultura*, *Juventuts Musicals* organize a course in chamber music, violin, viola, cello and piano. In July and August a series of international concerts is organized by the Sta. María Organ Foundation and, in the summer, organ recitals are given each morning and one afternoon per week. In August, summer concerts are held in the church at Fornells and, in the chapel or cloister of the Convent of Socors in Ciutadella, both singing and organ auditions are held throughout the year by the **Capella Davídica**. (Here the voice of the world-famous, Ciutadella-born baritone *Joan Pons*, currently considered among the world's finest, was trained.) Among other activities, they organize the **International Organ Week** in the cathedral in February or March, and Easter, summer and Christmas concerts.

JAZZ

Although not such a long-standing tradition among the Menorcans, jazz does have a place in the island's musical scene. In great part this is due to the large number of British residents who, over the years, have created and maintained this interest. From Easter until November, jazz sessions are held in the **Casino at St. Climent** on Tuesdays, and in the winter on Thursdays.

ROCK - POP

There are many amateur groups on the island and they give frequent performances. One of them, **Ja t'ho diré** by name, has become successful on a national level.

FOLK

The *Jota Menorquina* (folk song and dance), *Havaneres* (which date from the time of massive emigration to Cuba) and traditional songs form the basis of Menorca's folk culture. Several folk groups exist and perform at all the local *festes*.

LIVE MUSIC

Jazz, rock and folk concerts are held throughout the year in Maó, Ciutadella and other points of the island with the participation of both local and visiting musicians. In recent years, weekly performances in the Cloister del Carme form part of the **Estiu a Maó** (Summer in Maó) programme. In August, outdoor concerts are held in Sa Plaça in Alaior. In Maó harbour, the bar **Akelarre**, on Moll de Ponent has live jazz and rock at weekends and open-air shows are given at **S'Hort Nou** several times a week in summer. In the **Sa Sínia** bar in Es Castell, live performances are given all year round. In Ciutadella the **Bar Asere** on the harbour, also has live music. An alternative attraction is the **Bar Salon** in Es Castell where imitations of cabaret-style entertainment are performed in most original surroundings.

THEATRE

The recently renovated **Teatre Principal** and the **Sala Augusta** in Maó and the **Teatre des Born** in Ciutadella, are the centres of the island's ever-increasing theatrical activity.

The theatre is a long-standing Menorcan tradition as is made clear by the existence and yearly performance of local works that have their origins in the 19th century. What is more, each town can boast of having its own theatre which, since the beginning of the last century to the present day, has been witness to Menorcan enthusiasm for amateur dramatics. Despite the island's small population, local groups abound and their performances are well attended by their fellow townspeople. The old-established **Orfeó Maonés** and the **Delfí Serra** and **St. Miquel** groups from Ciutadella have a long tradition. **La Clota-Groc** and **Mô Teatre** are more recently formed, the latter producing their own works. The *Aules de Teatre* (theatrical classes) have, in recent years, enabled actors to maintain a high level of interpretative skills.

LITERATURE

Menorca's contribution to Catalan and European culture has been quite considerable, although it remains comparatively unknown to the public in general. After the foundation in 1778 of the *Societat Maonesa de Cultura*, there was intense activity in this field within the enlightened trends of the times. Many members of this group studied in the south of France, such as **Joan Ramis i Ramis**, the leading exponent of Catalan neoclassic drama whose works include *"Lucrècia"* (1769), in defence of republican liberties, *"Arminda"* and *"Rosaura o el més constant amor"*. At this time, works by Molière, Goldoni, Metastasio etc., were translated on the island and linguistic treatises published, such as the *Principis de lectura*

menorquina, in which the author **Febrer i Cardona** clearly defined the unity of the vernacular language within Catalan territories. Scientific literature was particularly represented by the work of **Dr. Orfila i Rotger** (1787-1853) who studied chemistry and medicine in Paris and whose studies on toxicology enjoyed great prestige. He was physician to Louis XVIII of France and chair of chemistry at the University of Paris.

In the 20th century, the famous *Folklore menorquí de la pagesia* by **Francesc d'Albranca** is one of the best-known works and the *Revista de Menorca*, published since 1888 by the Scientific, Literary and Artistic Athaeneum, is highly considered in literary circles. The *Obra Cultural Balear* is the association dedicated to the production and diffusion of the *Enciclopèdia de Menorca*, a thematic encyclopaedia published in fascicles of which several volumes have been completed to date.

Contemporary fiction and poetry is also represented on the island by **Gumersind Riera**, **Ponç Pons** and **Pau Faner**, who, between them, have won both local and national literary awards. All the forementioned works can be found in the island's book-shops along with any new publications by native writers.

A curious place to immerse ourselves in the world of books is the **Café-Librería La Torre de Papel**, in Ciutadella, Camí de Maó, 46. A cosy, pleasant atmosphere invites us to combine the pleasure of reading with that of a hot drink. Here we will find both new and secondhand books in several languages.

RECOMMENDED READING

• Arxiduc Lluís Salvador d'Àustria. **La isla de Menorca**. Facsimile editions of volumes VI i VII of *"Die Balearen in wort und bild"*. "Sa Nostra" 1982.
• Armstrong, John. **Historia de la isla de Menorca**. Edit. Nura 1978.
• Ballester, Pere. **De re cibaria** *(cocina, pastelería y repostería menorquina)* Edit. Puig, 1986.
• Camps i Mercadal, F. (Francesc d'Albranca). **Folklore Menorquí**. 1987.
• Cao Barredo, M. **Flowers of Menorca**. G.O.B. 1996.
• Catxot, Santi, i Escandell, Raúl. **Birds of Menorca**. G.O.B. 1994.
• Faner, Pau. **Flor de sal**. Destino 1986.
• Florit, F. i Sauleau, L. **Pedreres de Marès**. Líthica. 1995.
• Garrido, Carlos. **Menorca mágica**. Olañeta, 1990.
• Lafuente, Lorenzo. **Menorca, costumbres i paisajes**. Edit. Nura, 1975.
• Martorell, Josep. **Guia d'arqui-tectura de Menorca**. La Gaia Ciència. 1980.
• Mascaró Pasarius, Josep. **Geografía e Historia de Menorca**. (5 volums). Menorca. 1980/84.
• Mascaró Pasarius, Josep. **Las taulas**. Edit. Al-thor. 1983.
• Mata, Micaela. **Conquestes i reconquestes de Menorca**. Editorial 62. 1974.
• Mata, Micaela. **Menorca Británica**. I.M.E. 1994.
• Nicolás Mascaró, Joan C. de. **Guia des Camí de Cavalls de Menorca**. Triangle Postals. 1997.
• Nicolás Mascaró, Joan C. de. **Talaies i torres de defensa costanera**. I.M.E. 1994.
• Pallarès, Virgínia i Taltavull, Enric. **Guía Náutica Menorca**. Virgínia Pallarès. 1992.
• Pla, Josep. **Mallorca, Menorca e Ibiza**. Destino. 1950.
• Plantalamor Massanet, Lluís. **L'arquitectura prehistòrica i protohistòrica de Menorca**. Govern Balear. Treballs del Museu de Menorca, n. 13.
• Pons, Guillermo. **Historia de Menorca**. Menorca, 1977.
• Pons, Ponç. **Memorial de Tabarka**. Cruïlla, 1993.
• Riudavets i Tuduri, Pedro. **Historia de la Isla de Menorca** (1888) 2 volums. Al-Thor. 1983.

• Sabrafin, Gabriel. **Cuentos fabulosos y leyendas de las islas**. Olañeta, 1988.
• Sintes i de Olivar, **M. Pascual Calbó Calders, un pintor menorquín en la Europa Ilustrada**. "Sa Nostra". 1987.
• Vidal, Toni. **Menorca tot just ahir**. Triangle Postals, 2000.
• Vuillier, Gaston. **Les Illes Oblidades**. Edit. Moll, 1973.
• VV.AA. **Guia Arqueològica de Menorca**. C.I.M. 1984.
• VV.AA. **La ciutat des del carrer**. Ateneu de Maó. 1983.
• VV.AA. **La mar i Menorca**. *(La pintura a Menorca del segle XVIII a l'actualitat)*. Ajuntament de Ciutadella. 1993.
• VV.AA. Quaderns Xibau. **Col.lecció de Poesía Contemporània**. I.M.E. 1990/95.
• VV.AA. **Menorca, Reserva de la Biosfera**. "Sa Nostra". 1994.
• VV.AA. **Vives Llull**. "Sa Nostra" 1993.

HANDICRAFTS

Today, the traditional handicrafts of local origin still in production on the island comprise, in the main, of pottery and the making of *avarques*, typical peasant sandals. However, basketmaking, costume jewellery, leather work, textile and paper serigraphy are still carried out. Traditional Menorcan pottery is characterized by its use of local raw materials and the distinctive forms of the finished articles. Some of the most unusual are: pitchers, bottles, clay pipes with wooden mouthpieces, glazed bowls, demijohns, drinking and feeding troughs for farm animals. At his workshop at 12 C/Curniola, in Ciutadella, **Artur Gener** makes pottery following an old family tradition, and in Maó harbour at 10 Moll de Ponent, the **Lora Buzón** brothers sell both traditional and contemporary designs. Customers can watch the whole process, from potter's wheel to end result, in the workshop on view to the public.
In the case of the *avarques* we have mentioned previously, although they are found on sale all over the island, it is increasingly difficult to come into direct contact with the craftsmen who make them. **Can Servera** at 3 C/Metge Camps, Es Mercadal and **Can Doblas artesania** workshop at 1 C/Fred, Ferreries are exceptions. Other examples of local handicrafts can be found at the outdoor markets which take place daily in the summer and weekly the rest of the year: **Ses Voltes** and **S'Esplanada** (Maó), **Baixada Campllonch** (Ciutadella harbour), **Baixada Cales Fonts** (Es Castell) and the handicraft markets of Es Mercadal and Alaior. On Saturday mornings an interesting market is held in Ferreries where local farmers sell products such as honey, cheese, jam and preserves. Shoes and other leather goods of very high quality can be bought at the manufacturer's own outlets where, theoretically, the prices are lower than in the shopping centres. There are several of them on the outskirts of Ciutadella and on the main roads, and factory tours can be arranged by appointment. It is still possible to have shoes handmade to measure at a competitive price but this may not be practical for short-term visitors as it is quite a lengthy process as befits such a specialised handicraft.

ANTIQUES

The fact that antique dealers are to be found in most of the towns is hardly surprising on an island that has been enriched throughout its history by contributions from many different cultures. From the ancient civilizations, the remains of the Talayotic era that form part of Menorca's unique and protected archaeological heritage are the first examples, and are followed by Phoenician amphoras retrieved from the sea bed and Roman objects that have been discovered in the course of excavation and building work. Not to be forgotten are the fossils, nature's own "antiques", brought to light after millennia by the erosion of the elements. The British and French dominations left in their wake an important legacy of characteristic everyday objects which, in the course of time, have become sought-after antiques. A prime example is the 18th century Chippendale and Sheraton furniture imported, in the main, during the last British occupation. (Although this was the briefest of the three, the influence exerted by the English was greater and more far-reaching than in the past.) The furniture found its way, over the years, through inheritance or sale, into homes of all social levels. Occasionally, authentic pieces can still be found for sale. Even locally-made rustic furniture came under the English influence and is more refined and sophisticated than its counterparts elsewhere. Many other decorative objects, paintings, trinkets and valuables of varied origins, dating principally from the 18th and 19th centuries, can be found in the antique shops that are tucked away all over the island, particularly in Maó and Ciutadella. In the past, Menorca had been a collector's paradise, but nowadays the prices have become more in step with the market in general and bargains are unlikely. A monthly, public auction is held in St. Lluís where a truly heterogeneous selection of items is put up for sale at quite reasonable prices. Even to the uninitiated, any of these establishments can offer a fascinating insight into the traditions and life-style of the island in years gone by.

FESTIVITIES

The horse is the undisputed symbol of the *festes* of Menorca and we have already mentioned those of Ciutadella and Maó. They are held in honour of the patron saint of the town and give rise to sporting and cultural activities as well as religious celebrations. The first note of the *tambor i es flabiol* (the drum and the pipe) is the anxiously awaited sound that signals the start of the **colcada** or procession. With the exception of Ciutadella, where centuries-old rituals surround and determine the course of the festivities which reach their climax with the **Jocs des Pla** tournament, the **colcada** and **jaleo** take place on the afternoon of the saint's day and the following morning. In recent years, the old tradition of the **corregudes des Cós** or horse racing in the street, has been revived in Maó and the townspeople take part enthusiastically.

Festivities in honour of the patron saints are not the only fêtes that are celebrated. As befits a Mediterranean culture, Menorcans maintain many Christian and pagan traditions of which we give details here:

CALENDAR OF FESTIVITIES

JANUARY

St. Anthony's Day (patron saint of Menorca) in commemoration of the conquest of the island by Alfons III.
16th Street parties in Maó, Es Castell, St. Lluís and Mercadal
17th Activities in all the towns. In Ciutadella a traditional market is held in Pl. de l'Hospital and on the 19th a gastronomic fête in Ciutadella.

FEBRUARY, MARCH, APRIL.

Carnival. Movable between February and March. Fancy dress balls and processions of floats in all the towns.

Particularly original are the Black and White Ball in Es Migjorn and the *Ball de ses Tauletes* at the Casino Nou in Ciutadella, both on the Monday.
Easter. Movable. Religious ceremonies and processions all over the island.
Of particular interest:
Good Friday. The Procession of the Holy Burial in Maó and the procession in Es Migjorn of very ancient origin.
Easter Saturday. The Sacred Concert at Ciutadella cathedral with religious ceremonies that conclude with the Foc Nou in the cathedral square.
Easter Sunday. Procession of the *Encontre* in Maó and Es Migjorn. In Ciutadella at noon, a bonfire set alight by shots from a blunderbuss. In St. Lluís, Es Castell, St. Climent, Alaior and Mercadal, choir singing in the streets.
Whitsun. Movable. Traditional outings and picnics in the country and beaches from Ciutadella and Ferreries.

MAY

1st Sunday In Ferreries, cakes and pastries are blessed and sold in benefit of the parish. This is an ancient tradition that has only recently been reinstated.
15th St. Isidore's Day. Patron saint of farmers. Religious and sporting events at the Hermitage of Fàtima.
24th or the following Sunday. Procession of Maria Auxiliadora in Ciutadella. Religious ceremony and procession through the old part of the city. At Sa Contramurada, a concert by the Municipal Band and a street dance.

JUNE

Dia des Be. On the Sunday prior to St. John's Day, a sheep, adorned with coloured ribbons is carried through the streets accompanied by a piper to announce the beginning of the festivities.
23rd-24th. Vespers at the church of St. Joan de Missa, followed by

medieval tournaments and processions, demonstrations of equestrian skills at the *Jocs des Pla*.
29th St. Peter's Day (or the following weekend). Festivities, games and dancing in Maó harbour and regattas featuring old sailing and rowing boats.

JULY

9th Commemoration of the Turkish assault on Ciutadella in 1558. The **Act of Constantinople** is read in public and the *Junta de Caixers* is chosen for the St. John festivities of the following year.
10th St. Christopher's Day festivities where vehicles are blessed.
15th-16th The image of the Virgen of Carmen is carried around the harbours of Maó, Ciutadella and Fornells by a procession of boats of all kinds that are decorated with lights and garlands of flowers.
24th-25th St. James's Day festivities in Es Castell.
3rd weekend St. Martin's Day festivities in Mercadal.
4th weekend St. Anthony's Day festivities in Fornells.
5th weekend (or first in August) St. Christopher's Day festivities in Es Migjorn.

AUGUST

1st weekend St. Gaietà's Day festivities in Llucmassanes.
1st weekend after the 10th, St. Lawrence's Day festivities in Alaior.
3rd weekend St. Clement's Day festivities in St. Climent.
23rd-25th St. Bartholomew's Day festivities in Ferreries.
Last weekend St. Louis's Day festivities in St. Lluís.

SEPTEMBER

7th-8th Our Lady of Grace festivities in Maó, another chance to see processions, horses and *jaleo*.
29th St. Michael's Day festivities in Es Migjorn with horses and *jaleo* every fifth year.

NOVEMBER

1st All Saints' Day. Traditional doughnuts with honey are sold all over the island.

DECEMBER

25th Nativity plays are performed in several towns. Exhibitions of crèches and Nativity dioramas in Maó and in Ciutadella at the Seminary and Sta. Clara church.
31st The New Year is celebrated at midnight by the ringing of bells in town squares and public dances.

OTHER FOLK TRADITIONS

CODOLADES

These are popular poetic compositions, usually of a satiric nature, whose metre differs in Menorca from other places. They tend to make reference to local or collective situations and affairs.

GLOSATS

Poetic compositions improvised by different people in turn, accompanied by the guitar. Both these examples of traditional folk culture have been kept alive, in great part, thanks to groups from Ciutadella and Ferreries who periodically give performances all over the island.

SPORT

IN RECENT YEARS MUCH HAS BEEN DONE TO IMPROVE THE QUALITY OF THE ISLAND'S SPORTS FACILITIES AND, TODAY, NEARLY ALL THE TOWNS HAVE THEIR OWN SPORTS GROUNDS. MANY HOTELS AND URBANIZATIONS ALSO HAVE INSTALLATIONS.

CRICKET

The large number of British residents on the island has given rise to the formation of a cricket club, the **Menorca Cricket Club** (or M.C.C.) to be found on the Biniparrell road, near St. Lluís. It is the only grass cricket pitch in Spain.

GOLF

There is a nine-hole golf course at on right hand side of the Fornells road. The high price the environment pays in return for these facilities is subject of considerable controversy and has prevented more courses from being developed.

HORSE SPORTS

We have already mentioned the important role the horse has always played in Menorcan society. The indigenous race of black horses is characterized by its medium stature and the long, straight profile of the head. Efforts are being made to encourage their breeding.
The **Maó hippodrome** lies on the road to St. Lluís and there is another in Ciutadella at **Torre del Ram**. Race meetings are held regularly and feature a variety of trotting races unique to the island. Betting is permitted.
The riding clubs belonging to the Federació Hípica Balear (Tel.971 37 82 20) are only concerned with classical Menorcan training, but also have horses for beginners to practise in the stables or to take out for rides.
Club Escola Menorquina. Ferreries to Cala Galdana road. From June to October, exhibitions every Wednesday and Sunday at 20h 30.
Tel. 971 15 50 59.
Club Hípic Alaior. Es Cos.
Tel. 971 37 82 43.
C H. Ferreries. On the road to Es Migjorn.
Tel. 971 37 42 03.
C. H. Ciutadella. Camí des Caragol.
Tel. 971 38 26 73.
C. H. Maó. Camí de Talatí.
Tel. 626 084 352.
C. H. Sa Creueta. (Es Migjorn) c/ Figuerenya, 18. Tel. 971 37 02 58.
C. H. Ses Ramones. (Es Mercadal) Maó-Ciutadella road.
Tel. 971 37 50 54.
Escola Eqüestre Menorquina. (Ciutadella) Camí des Caragol.
Tel. 971 38 34 25.
Grup Cavallers Cuadras Bintaufa. (Maó) c/ Cos de Gràcia, 56.
Tel. 971 35 23 47.

Other related options are the **Pony Club** (for children only), in the Sant Tomàs urbanisation, Es Migjorn Gran, Tel. 971 37 03 70, and the **Hort de Llucaitx Park** on the Maó to Fornells road (near the Son Parc turning).
Tel. 629 392 894.

TENNIS

Tennis is a popular game on the island and there are several schools and coaches who give private lessons and every town has its own cour.
The **Tennis Club S'Algar** is one of the most attractive as the courts are surrounded by a pinewood which affords welcome shade all year round. They also have artificial grass paddle tennis courts.

OTHER ALTERNATIVES:

At the **St. Lluís Flying Club**, light aircraft flights can be arranged and offer the chance to discover the island from the air. They also have a go-kart circuit.

The **GOB** (Grup Balear d'Ornitologia) offers another, alternative way to discover the island. They organize excursions for limited groups with country walks, trips to beaches and the archaeological routes which are of interest to both amateur ornithologists and nature lovers in general.
They can be contacted at 138 Camí des Castell, Maó, from 9h-15h, or by phoning 971 35 07 62.
Two sports are unique to Menorca, and one of them is exclusive to just St. Lluís. This is **La Bolla**, a kind of indoor bowling which probably originated during the French domination. It can be watched in the bar La Bolla, 56 Es Cós, St. Lluís. The second is **Joc Maonés**, more a kind of martial art of unknown origin than a game. The practice of this curious art was unique to only a few *aficionados* and their *maestros* who passed the tradition by word-of-mouth from generation to generation until quite recently when public interest has been revived and supported by local institutions. It is renowned for the singular elegance of the steps, tocs which increase in intensity prior to the combat itself, rodar. The participants are not in danger of injury as their optimum physical preparation is closely controlled by the teachers.

NAUTICAL SPORTS

As far as these activities are concerned, the possibilities seem endless. From sailing boats to pedaloes, passing through windsurf boards and motorboats, almost every kind of craft is available for hire. Until recently, despite the idyllic conditions for canoeing offered by Menorca's protected ports, this sport was not practiced on the island. Now, however, canoes are for hire from **Katakayak,** Fornells, on the promenade, from the **Diving Centre Cala Torret,** and at some other beaches. Excellent nautical sports facilities and services exist in Maó, Ciutadella and Fornells and, also, in many holiday centres. Visitors should bear in mind, however, that in the high season the demand for craft for hire is far greater than the supply. If you wish to focus your holiday in Menorca in this direction, arrangements should be made in advance and it would be wise to obtain one of the nautical guides that are available on the market. Whether you wish to hire your own craft or just take a short trip, the following information may be of assistance.

Maó harbour: Sailing and motorboat hire at **Menmar** and **Menorca Nàutic,** both on Moll de Llevant.

Years ago, the Maoneses who lived or holidayed on the opposite shore of the port would commute to and fro on the old *Barca d'en Reynes.* Nowadays, the increase in marine traffic, largely due to the ever-expanding tourist industry, has drastically altered the harbour's atmosphere but it still remains an enchanting setting, particularly in the early morning and evening. There are several boats that do pleasure trips around the harbour with running commentaries in several languages. They are to be found next door to the Trasmediterranea building. Another, smaller taxi-boat is also available and also a glass-bottomed boat which offers views of the marine floor. The depth of Maó harbour, 20 to 30 metres in most places, does not permit the best of visibility.

Es Castell: Boat trips around the port also start from here at midday.

The **Llatzeret** island can only be visited in groups and by prior arrangement. Tel. 971 36 25 87.

Es Grau: A small cabin-cruiser runs a shuttle service to the Illa d'en Colom.

We have already mentioned Fornells harbour as a nautical sports paradise. There is also a taxi-boat and motor and rowing boat rental service at **Servi-Nàutic Menorca.** Sailing boats, catamarans and windsurf equipment can be found at **Windsurf Fornells,** and at **Club Nàutic ses Salines,** an important sailing schooll.

Ciutadella and Cala Galdana: Boat trips can be taken to the south coast beaches and some are glass-bottomed which, in this instance, is a very attractive alternative, given the variety and beauty of the marine floor in this area. In Ciutadella harbour there are facilities for boat rental such as **Sports Massanet** at Marina 66, Moll Comercial.

There are diving clubs in S'Algar, **S'Algar Diving** and in Binibequer, **Centro de Buceo Cala Torret.** In Fornells, **Menorca Diving Club** and in Port d'Addaia, **Ulmo Diving.** In Son Xoriguer and Son Bou, **Sub Menorca Centros de Buceo** and, in Ciutadella, **Ciutadella Diving.**

For further information contact:

The **Federación de Actividades Subacuáticas.** Francesc de Borja Moll, 21. Ciutadella.

Federación de Vela. Av. Menorca, 96 4º A. Maó. Tel. 971 36 39 89

Two associations exist in Menorca with the aim of protecting the island's marine heritage: *Amics des Port de Maó* and *Amics de la Mar de Menorca.* Between them they aim to conserve the ports and the coastline, and safeguard the long-standing cultural and ethnological traditions.

ACCOMMODATION

Apart from the hotels, appartments and holiday accommodation in general, other possibilities, of a more environmentally-friendly nature are also available. There are a few small hotels that maintain the traditional style of rural architecture and, as a result, form a harmonious part of the surrounding countryside. Their very size and nature makes advance reservation an absolute necessity. A few examples are:

Hostal Biniali At S'Ullestrar, near St. Lluís.
Tel. 971 15 17 24,
Fax. 971 15 03 52.
A renovated mansion, laid back from the main road, with swimming pool and gardens. Nine well-appointed, elegantly furnished bedrooms and pleasant surroundings.

Hotel Almirante Near Es Castell on the main road from Maó.
Tel. 971 36 27 00. A remodelled 18th century house where Admiral Collingwood resided in Lord Nelson's time. Gardens, tennis court, swimming pool and, allegedly, a haunted room.

S'Engolidor 3 Major St. Es Migjorn. Tel. 971 37 01 93. An old farmhouse now integrated into the town. Boardinghouse with just four simple, but comfortable bedrooms, and a restaurant well-known for the quality of its traditional Menorcan cuisine.

Asociación Hotelera de Menorca, Information and bookings: telephone 971 36 10 03. e-mail: ashome@infotelecom.es and website: www.infotelecom.es/ashome

RURAL TOURISM

Just recently, a new concept of holiday accommodation has been introduced on the island. Rural tourism offers visitors the opportunity of staying in country houses that have been adapted for this purpose and we list here a few of those that are already open.

Lloc de Binisaïd. Near Ferreries on the Cala Galdana road. Farmhouse in one of the most luxuriantly wooded areas of the island.
Tel. 971 15 50 63/971 35 23 03.

Son Triay Nou. On the Cala Galdana road, 2 km. out of Ferreries. Four bedrooms, swimming pool, tennis court, garden and pleasant rural surroundings.
Tel. 971 15 50 78/ 971 36 04 46.

Lloc de Biniatram. Near Ciutadella on the Cala Morell road. A stately home which offers the possibility of enjoying the life-style and gastronomy of rural Menorca. Four bedrooms, swimming pool and tennis court. Tel-971 38 31 13.

Lloc de Sant Tomàs. In Ciutadella on the Camí Vell de Maó, km.3. Three bedrooms. Guests have the chance to go on horseback rides and sample typical Menorcan cuisine.
Tel. 971 18 80 51.

Alcaufar Vell. Sant Lluís to Alcalfar road, km 7,3. Four double rooms in the rural surroundings of the eastern part of the island. Various facilities such as bicycle and horseriding, rambling... Tel. 971 15 18 74.

Matxaní Gran. Sant Climent to Binidalí road. Six bedrooms.
Tel. 971 15 33 00.

Talatí de Dalt. Camí de Talatí (Maó). Four bedrooms. Tel. 971 37 11 58. For more information and bookings contact: **Asociación de Agroturismo Balear,** 971 72 75 08. e-mail: agroturismo@mallorcanet.com

Son Tretze, in St. Lluís,with eight bedrooms and a meeting hall offers the same style of accommodation within the town itself. Binifadet, 20.
Tel. 971 15 33 00.

Another possibility lies in renting houses directly from their owners who use them only part of the time as holiday homes, either on the coast if the proprietors choose to stay in town, or vice versa.

Although no sleeping accommodation is provided, **Lloc de Binisues** on the road to Ciutadella, 31 km. from Maó on the turning to Els Alocs, is worth mentioning for its restaurant, traditional architecture and permanent exhibition of antiques and rural curiosities. Tel.971 37 37 28.

CAMPING

Camping on the island is very problematic as local people have never been well-disposed to the use of their land for this purpose. There are only two camping sites, both well-equipped, close to the beach and with swimming pools.

Càmping S'Atalaia. Four km. from Ferreries on the Cala Galdana road. Open in the summer, just 3 km. from the beach with all kinds of services and swimming pool. Communicated by bus with Ferreries and the rest of the island and also Cala Galdana.
Tel. 971 37 42 32/971 37 30 95.

Càmping Son Bou. Conveniently and centrally situated on the Sant Jaume road, 3,5 km. from Alaior and just 2,5 km. from the beach. Mini-golf, swimming pool, solarium, sports facilities in pleasant surroundings.
Tel/Fax. 971 37 26 05.

A number of country houses exist where youth organizations are allowed to use the sleeping, kitchen and bathroom facilities. In the event of there being vacancies, which is not probable in the high season, they are also available to private groups or families:

Es Pinaret. Near Ciutadella.
Tel. 971 38 10 50.

Torre de Son Ganxo and **Campament de Biniparratx.** Near St. Lluís.
Tel. 971 17 10 93/971 15 15 16.

St. Llorenç de Binixems. Near Alaior at the hermitage. Tel. 971 37 11 07.

Es Canaló. Near Ferreries at the beginning of the Algendar barranc Tel. 971 37 40 72.

St. Joan de Missa. Near Ciutadella at the hermitage. Tel. 971 38 10 82/971 38 13 06.

GASTRONOMY

We have already mentioned gin and cheese, as the most emblematic of Menorca's products, but the island has much more to offer in the way of gastronomy. "*De Re Cibaria*" is a classic book of Menorcan cooking and is an excellent guide for those who wish to make an in depth discovery of the island's cuisine, whether in the form of every day dishes or other, sometimes archaic specialities. The simple tasting of local food suffices to identify its sources: the basic ingredients available, fruit of the land or the sea, and the influence of the different successive occupations (Arab, British and French) on their preparation. The origin of mayonnaise has been the source of international dispute between Menorcans and the French for centuries.

Oliaigo (literally oil and water), is a simple dish considered to be ideal for all seasons, eaten cold in summer and hot in winter. It is often served accompanied by figs. The basic ingredients are onion, garlic, green peppers and tomato cooked in a deep earthenware dish and served with fine slices of dry, white bread.

Caldereta de llagosta (lobster stew), is the island's most famous dish but was regarded, before the arrival of tourism, as simple fare which the fishermen would prepare on board their boats. Today it is considered as food fit for a king.

Calderetes are also made with other kinds of fish and shellfish.

Arròs de la terra (Rice of the earth) is a peasant dish made of ground maize, and baked aubergines. All the above-mentioned are traditional recipes whose simple ingredients tell us much of the limited natural resources of the island in years gone by, and man's ingenuity in transforming them into appetising dishes.

From the sea, apart from the wealth of fish caught in the surrounding waters, come **escopinyes**, sea dates, and **corns**. Different types of sausage are made on the island: **sobrassada**, **camot** and **carn i xua** and both

savoury and sweet pastries such as the **formatjades** and **coques** of Ciutadella, the famous **amargos**, **carquinyols** and **torró crema**t of Es Mercadal and **crespells**, **pastissets** and **ensaïmades** to be found everywhere.

Restaurants on the island are many and varied in quality, style and cuisine. Our intention is to give a few representative examples which, in no way, should be considered as anything more than a guideline.

TRADITIONAL COOKING

Good traditional food can be found at **Ca n'Aguedet**, 23 C/Lepant, Es Mercadal, and at **S'Engolidor**, Es Migjorn, which we have already mentioned in the previous section.

FISH AND SHELLFISH

There are many restaurants specialized in fish and seafood in general. At Cala Mesquida, **Cap Roig**, offers a wonderful view of the coastline. In Maó harbour, despite the ever-increasing number of restaurants, there are not many dedicated to fish. On Moll de Llevant, **Es Fosquet** being an exception. At Cales Fonts, **Trebol**, one of the busiest of the many quayside establishments and **Can Delio**. In Ciutadella, among others, **Tritón** and **Cafe Balear,** both in the harbour. In Fornells, **Es Cranc**, 29 C/Escoles, and **Es Pla**, **Cranc Pelut, Can Miquel Es Port,** on the sea front. Another style of restaurant typical of the island can be found in old farmhouses where the atmosphere tends to be informal and the surroundings traditional and simple.

Similar establishments also exist in the towns: **Andaira,** 61 C/ des Forn, Tel. 971 36 68 17, in the centre of Maó, is set in an elegant town house with tables in the garden. In Ciutadella, **Es Racó des Palau,** 3 C/Palau an old renovated bakery. In Mercadal, **Ca n'Olga**, Pont de Macarrana, tel. 971 37 54 59 and **Molí des Racó**, set in a restored windmill. In Es Migjorn Gran, **Bar Chic**, 7 C/ Major and, in Ferreries, **Liorna**, 9 C/ Dalt, serves good pizzas in a charming setting.

Of the farmhouse restaurants, many are situated in the Sant Lluís area: **La Caraba**, at S'Ullastrar 78 with both indoor dining rooms and a charming garden terrace, Tel. 971 15 06 82, and nearby, at Nº 46, **Villa Madrid** set in a colonial-style mansion, Tel. 971.15.04.64.

All around the island's coastline there are places to eat and drink just a few steps away from the sea (some very informal and others of a more serious nature). The style of food varies from the simplest to the most elaborate. Four km. from Sant Lluís, **Restaurante Son Ganxo** near a secluded cove, with swimming pool, terrace and indoor restaurant and **Es Caragol** between Biniancolla and Cala Torret.

TRANSPORT

BY PLANE

Iberia flies regularly between Menorca, Barcelona, Mallorca and Valencia all year. At Christmas, Easter and in the summer, services are increased owing to the high demand. Information: Tel. 971 36 90 15. Reservations: Tel. 971 36 56 73. Other companies offer regular flights to both Barcelona and Palma which connect to other destinations: **Air Europe**, information and bookings, Tel. 971 15 70 31 /902 240 042; and **Air Nostrum**, Tel. 902 400 500 **Norestair.** Air taxi and air ambulance. Tel. 608.530.606 or 971 35 13 07. The airport is on the PM-703 Maó–St. Climent road. Tel. 971 15 70 00.

BY BOAT

Trasmediterránea covers the line Maó-Barcelona twice a week in winter and more frequently during holiday seasons. The trip takes about eight hours. Once a week they sail to Mallorca and then on to Valencia. Information: 971 36 60 50 Reservations: 971 36 29 50 **Iscomar** sails from Ciutadella-Alcúdia twice daily. This three-hour trip is an ideal way to visit Mallorca, taking one's own car. Tel. 971 48 42 16. **Cape Balear** also communicates Ciutadella and Cala Rajada (also in Mallorca) twice daily but only carries passengers. Tel. 902 100 444. **Universal Naviera** offers quick trips to Barcelona and Alcúdia by *Turbocat* catamaran. Tel. 902 181 888

BY BUS

Transportes Menorca runs a regular bus service from Maó to Ciutadella every thirty minutes during the day and to Es Castell, St. Lluís, Es Migjorn, Ferreries, St. Climent and Fornells at varying times. During the summer, additional routes cover some of the urbanizations (Alcalfar, Punta Prima, Binibèquer, es Canutells, Cala en Porter, Son Bou, Sant Tomàs and Cala Galdana). The station for the main Maó-Ciutadella line is in the Esplanada, Maó. (Tel. 971 36 03 61) and at 8 C/Barcelona, Ciutadella. Tel. 971 38 03 93.
Autos Fornells S.A. From Maó to Fornells and the built-up beaches of the north east coast (Arenal d'en Castell, Son Parc, Platges de Fornells and es Grau). Tel. 971 37 66 21.
Autocars Torres connects Ciutadella with Sa Caleta, Santandria, Cala Blanca, Cala en Bosc, Son Xoriguer, Cala en Blanes, Los Delfines and Cala en Forcat. Tel. 971 38 64 61.
In the *Agenda* section of the Menorca newspaper, daily up-to-date information is given on bus, plane and boat times as well as petrol stations, on duty chemists and an entertainments guide.

BY CAR

The speed limits on the island are 90 km.p.h. on the main roads, 50 km.p.h. in the towns, and 30 km.p.h. on the country lanes. On these narrow lanes, extreme precaution is recommended and the use of the horn is advisable on the frequent blind bends. There are, of course, many exceptions to these speed limits but they are always clearly signposted. Not many bicycle lanes exist on the island and many busy roads have no pavements for pedestrians. Seat belts are compulsory on all roads as are crash helmets for motorcyclists. Drinking and driving is now heavily penalised and a breathalyser test can be demanded of any driver, even if no offence has been committed. Severe

fines and/or loss of licence will follow a result of more than 0,5gr/litre. Serious accidents have become more frequent in recent years, due in part to visiting drivers' belief that the roads here are not dangerous Precaution and respect for other road users are the only solution and, above all, do remember to keep to the right. Both international and local car rental companies have offices at the airport and in some of the larger towns. In the high season, the demand far outreaches the supply and bookings must be made well in advance. Package holidays that include the price of a car are the most economic solution. Motor-cycles and bicycles can also be hired from a number of companies all over the island.

MEDICAL ATTENTION

The **Virgen de Monte Toro** is the island's public health hospital. C/ Barcelona, Maó, Tel. 971 15 77 00. In case of emergency call 061. Each area of the island has a health centre which also deal with emergencies.
Dalt St. Joan, in Maó, C/ Fornells 107. Tel. 971 35 29 90.
Es Banyer, in Alaior, C/ Mestre Duran . Tel. 971 37 29 17/971 37 29 31.
Canal Celat, in Ciutadella, C/ St. Antoni Mª Claret, Tel. 971 48 01 11.
A service specially created for women can be consulted at Dalt St. Joan at the above address. Tel. 971 35 29 88.
Cruz Roja (Red Cross) First-aid stations on the main beaches Private medical attention is available at **Policlínica Verge de Gràcia**, C/ Vives Llull 6, Maó, Tel. 971 36 68 60, and **Clinica Menorca**, C/ Canonge Moll, Ciutadella, Tel. 971 48 05 05.

AMBULANCE SERVICES

Emergencies:
Mobile unit   061
Red Cross:
Maó 971 36 11 80
Ciutadella 971 38 19 93

USEFUL TELEPHONES

Emergencies: 112

Fire brigade:
Maó 971 35 10 11
. . . .   971 36 39 61
Ciutadella 971 38 08 09
. . . .   971 38 07 87

Civil defence 971 36 33 53

Telegrams 971 36 38 95

Police:
National police   091
Municipal police   092
Civil guard   062

Radio taxi:
Maó, Alaior, Mercadal .   971 36 71 11
Ciutadella 971 38 28 96
Es Castell 971 36 27 79
Sant Lluís 971 15 06 41
Ferreries 971 37 34 84

Consell Insular 971 35 15 15

Tourist:
Tourist information:
Maó 971 36 37 90
. . . .   971 36 08 79
Ciutadella 971 38 26 93
Tourist Board 971 36 23 77
Youth information 971 36 45 34

Town Halls:
Alaior 971 37 10 02
Ciutadella 971 38 10 50
Es Castell 971 36 51 93
Es Mercadal 971 37 50 02
Es Migjorn Gran 971 37 01 11
Ferreries 971 37 30 03
Maó 971 36 98 00
Sant Lluís 971 15 09 50

Consulates:
Great Britain: 971 36 33 73
. . . .   971 71 24 45
France: 971 35 43 87
Germany: 971 36 16 68
Holland: 971 35 43 63
Italy: 971 72 42 14